Wandering Close to Home

A Gay Son and His Feminist Mother's Journey to Transform Themselves and Their Family

By
Christopher Drajem
& Linda Drajem

NFB Publishing
Buffalo, New York

Copyright © 2019 Christopher Drajem & Linda Drajem

Printed in the United States of America

Wandering Close to Home: A Gay Son and His Feminist Mother's Journey to Transform Themselves and Their Family / Drajem, Christopher & Linda Drajem—1st Edition

ISBN: 978-09978317-4-0

1. Title.
2. Feminism.
    Feminists--Biography--20th Century
    Feminists--Family relationships--United States
    Feminists--United States--Biography
3. Gay Life.
    Gay men--Family relationships--United States
    Gay men--United States--Biography
    Catholic gays--United States--Biography
    Parents of gays

4. Authors, American
5. Drajem, Christopher & Linda Drajem

No part of this book may be reproduced or transmitted in any form by any means, electronic or mechanical, including photocopying, recording, or by any information storage and retrieval system without permission in writing by the author.

Cover Design by Euan Monaghan
Author photo by Nancy J. Parisi

NFB
NFB Publishing/Amelia Press
119 Dorchester Road
Buffalo, New York 14213
For more information visit Nfbpublishing.com

DISCLAIMER

The stories in these pages come from the memory of the authors. Some of the names of particular individuals have been changed. However, they have tried to be as truthful as possible in the retelling of events.

Wandering Close to Home
A Gay Son and His Feminist Mother's Journey to Transform Themselves and Their Family

Table of Contents

Introduction		13
Chapter 1	Linda: Maps	21
Chapter 2	Linda: Education from Life	31
Chapter 3	Linda: Becoming a Teacher	41
Chapter 4	Christopher: Different	51
Chapter 5	Christopher: Sin	65
Chapter 6	Christopher: Fear	77
Chapter 7	Linda: A Family Home	93
Chapter 8	A Note from Dad	107
Chapter 9	Christopher: Closet	111
Chapter 10	Christopher: Spring	121
Chapter 11	Linda: Becoming a Feminist Woman	135
Chapter 12	Christopher: Heading West	149
Chapter 13	Linda: Coming Out for a Mom	173
Chapter 14	Letter from Mark	185
Chapter 15	Linda: Teaching and Learning	189
Chapter 16	Christopher: Commitment	201
Chapter 17	Linda: Marriage	219
Chapter 18	Christopher: Parenting	229
Chapter 19	Linda: Grandparenting from a Distance	247
Chapter 20	Christopher: Seismic Shifts	255
Conclusion		269

To Bob, my yesterday, now, and forever guy.
And of course the four beautiful grandchildren,
Zoe, Isabella, Noah, and Jordan—these stories are for you
—Linda

For Patrick, my husband and partner.
And for Dad and Mark, who teach me so much about being a good man.
—Christopher

March 28, 1994

Dear Christopher,

As you might expect is has been a very different week for mom and I. There are a number of distorted thoughts running around in my head and I hope that this note makes sense to you. First, please know that I love you dearly and your decisions that you are may or my very thoughts or will not change my love for you.

[signature]

INTRODUCTION—Christopher

I feel like you've been gone a long time, and now you're home, and I very much need to know about your journey, even if it was and is painful. I love you very much, and I want to know about your life and share its pain and happiness.
   Letter from Mom, May 3, 1994

In the midafternoon of a cold March day in 1994, Mom and I sat in a coffee shop in Buffalo, the city where I was born and raised, and snuggled into our latte (me) and black tea (Mom). I had been living in Seattle since the previous fall, and I had not been home to see my parents since Christmas. Still, Mom and I jumped into a conversation both searing and easy; it was a dramatic turn and yet just one more intimate conversation between two adults trying to find their way. Over the past few years, we had spent hours in similar talks, discussing new poets we had found and troublesome students, movies we loved and politicians who drove us crazy. On this particular day, though, I took things in a different direction and said, "Mom, I'm gay."

In 1994, the year I came out, people still sent hand-written letters through the United States Postal Service. They arrived days later, especially if they had to travel across the country from Buffalo, New York, to Seattle. Dad often typed his, and he was the first to send me a letter, which opened like this:

> *As you might expect, it has been a different week for Mom and me. There are a number of disjointed thoughts running around in my head, and I hope this note makes some sense to you. First, please know that I love you dearly and your disclosure that you are gay in no way changes or will ever change my love for you.*

Filled with a sense of relief that I had shared a truth I had held inside for far too long, I cried reading Dad's letter in the dingy basement apartment where I lived. I counted on Mom and Dad's unconditional love, but it was comforting to see the tangible proof there, typed out in black and white.

The letters did include some questions and admissions of guilt. They reflect a couple struggling to come to terms with something they never thought too much about, something they never thought they would have to deal with from one of their sons. They discuss books that they had read, and the Parents and Friends of Lesbians and Gays (PFLAG) meeting they had attended. They discuss the happiness they recognized in my life since I had come out, and expressed the desire, as Mom put it in one letter, "to know the real you" and to seek "an opportunity to now be comfortable with the lifestyle that suits you."

The letters continued, and by the late 1990s, I suggested to Mom that, as writers, we should consider sharing our story. I had even found a book that inspired me. It was called *Not Like Other*

Boys: Growing Up Gay: A Mother and Son Look Back and it was written in 1996 by Marlene Fanta Shyer and Christopher Shyer. I sent Mom a copy for Mother's Day one year and inscribed it "Us next?" In an email, I expanded on my idea. We could chart the journey of our family from its traditional middle-class, Catholic Buffalo roots to my twist on the future Mom and Dad had expected for me and my brother. Instead of marrying a woman and having kids, I married a great guy, and we adopted two.

But the story of our family is not just the story of my coming out. It was Patrick, that great guy I married, who cut to the chase when I first mentioned a book. "I love you, honey," he said, "but your mom needs to tell the story of her journey as well, and how that impacted your family."

He was right, of course. When my brother, Mark, and I left for college, Mom decided that she wanted her career as a teacher to shift. She started to write poetry. She went back to school to work toward a Ph.D. in Women's Studies. For a good Catholic girl who was brought up on the traditional gender roles of the 1950s, her path was a radical departure, and it certainly had bumps and detours along the way.

The story Mom and I have set out to tell in this book is about our individual evolutions, how we pursued paths that were, for us, uncharted and filled with obstacles but that we knew instinctively we needed to undertake. It is also a story of our mutual support and encouragement. We decided to let one another in, to share the journey with one another and to become travelling partners.

Here is our travelogue.

INTRODUCTION—Linda

None of us can ever know the value of our lives, or how our separate and silent scribbling may add to the amenity of the world, if only by how radically it changes us, one and by one.
  Mary Karr, *The Art of Memoir*

When we started this writing project ten years ago, our focus was on how we had reshaped our gay and straight extended family. Our goal was and is to encourage other LGBTQ families that we can succeed in new and empowering ways. Not that we are perfect or things are perfect. No way. But some coming-out stories show the awful reactions of frightened parents. Our message is that it does not have to be this way. We have been lucky enough to live through an amazing time of change, an era of openness and honesty. That said, many challenges remain.

Since the nineties a great societal shift has taken place and we are part of it. Gays and lesbians decided they could not hide who they are, and their families learned that the issue of their sexuality did not change their love for them. I think there is a straight line running from Christopher's coming out in 1994 to the Supreme Court's decision on same-sex marriage in 2015. He was honest and straightforward with expressing who he is, which fundamentally impacted our family. He, like so many other LGBT persons, forced a vast social change, and our story is one of many in these last decades.

In addition, both Christopher and I are writers. We have been writing to each other since he came out. Over time our letters became emails and blog posts. After Christopher proposed this book it evolved in fits and starts. Christopher is a full-time teacher, a busy father of two and a committed husband. He is also an activist who does presentations to universities and prospective adoptive families on LGBTQ parenting. So his time is limited.

I have more time as a retired teacher, but my husband, Bob, and I travel a great deal, mostly to see our two adult sons and their families. At times the project also became too much for me. It took me to places I did not want to go. It was and is painful to read about how much Christopher suffered in high school and college.

Then, just a few years ago, Christopher said to me something like this: "It's your story, too. You have moved way beyond the path of your youth. You have become a feminist, a late-blooming Ph.D., and LGBTQ activist as well."

He went on to say that we have both been on journeys to selves far different from our beginnings. Perhaps anyone who has been around during the social upheavals of the last several decades can see themselves in how Christopher and I evolved.

For a very long time, I resisted the idea of a sort of collaborative memoir. I asked myself why anyone on earth, besides my family and friends, would be interested in me. That may still be true. But I am now convinced that both of us, son and mother, have been on somewhat parallel journeys shaped by the great cultural shifts in women's rights and gay rights. On those journeys, we have encouraged each other and been encouraged by Bob, my husband and partner for almost fifty-five years, and Mark, my older son and brave soul himself. Each of us in our own way has tried to contribute to these societal efforts to expand notions of what it means to be fully human, fully ourselves.

Consequently, dear reader, if you are to understand how my journey swerved from what it was supposed to be, you need to understand my origins. It has often been difficult for me to go back, to revisit early memories. For no one is the past always rosy, but if I hadn't gone back, my story would have been incomplete. So I start at the beginning.

Chapter 1
Linda: Maps

i am here waiting
remembering that
once as a child
i walked two
miles in my sleep
did I know
then where i
was going?
traveling. i'm
always traveling.
—Sonia Sanchez, "poem at thirty"

On the map of New York State, far to the west of Manhattan, there is the city of Buffalo sidestepping the Niagara River. At the northern most tip of this smaller metropolis my journey begins. Born in 1942, my mother said that I started World War II and that my sister Judy ended it with her birth in 1945. Not true of course. Mom was a great storyteller.

When I was born, Dad had just been hired at Bell Aircraft to help ship airplanes off to the war. We lived with my grandparents in Riverside, a neighborhood of stacked two family homes next to the river. My grandfather ran a small shoe-repair shop close by. The map of my life starts here.

We girls had lots of rules. Our world on our dead-end street was very circumscribed. We could not even ride our bikes off the street or walk to the park a few miles from our house. Of course, we were not expected to give an opinion or disagree with a grown-up. Such obstreperousness was met with a slap or two.

Our house was often filled with family. And even though my mom and grandma were not healthy, family dinners marked our lives. Christmas was the biggest celebration. On Christmas Eve, we all had to attend midnight Mass. Grandpa insisted on a big feast prior to that for my mother's brothers and their families, meatless by religious tradition. I remember seeing eels swimming in the bathtub as well as baskets of dried cod stacked like wood in the basement. Jars of spaghetti sauce in the fruit cellar that Mom and Grandma had sweated over in August were now cracked open and bubbling on the back burner. Christmas was a time for the men to relax with a glass of Chianti. For my mom and grandmother, who both suffered from arthritis, it was another day of labor.

Our extended family was the only Italian family in our neighborhood. Mom told me not to tell the neighbors what we ate, including odd items like snails. On one occasion the critters crawled out of a basket and invaded the whole basement. However, the scents wafting from our kitchen windows jimmied open in winter must have alerted them.

Easter was the next big feast. To celebrate, Mom and Grandma would make ravioli and lay out the little envelopes of dough to dry on Grandma's ancient oak table that filled her tiny dining room. Of course, we girls had to pitch in, rolling the pasta dough, cleaning up the floured boards, washing dishes. In our household, as soon as girls could hold a dishtowel, they were pressed into service.

Around the dining table, the men held court. But in the kitchen it was the women, especially after dinner washing pan after pan in hot billowy suds. Powerful were the whispered secrets, bubbling over the linen dishtowels used while drying the plain white dishes from Woolworth's five-and-dime. Secrets of pain carried under cotton aprons, the abortion gone bad, the breast burned by a husband's cigarette, the abandoned babies, and the lost aunts who lived by the docks. We girls imbibed the words as we scraped plates, scrubbed burned bits with Brillo pads and put sparkling dishes away. Those rumbling stories held such power.

They prefigured the tragedies I would learn about years later. One of my mother's aunts married a man who turned out to be a pedophile, though they did not use that word then. When we visited their home, my great aunt told my mother to be sure to keep him away from my sister and me and the other girl cousins. Another great aunt might show up with a black eye on occasion. The story was that she fell. Even my mother's brothers had their problems. One was a known womanizer. Another abandoned his two kids to an orphanage in Buffalo after his wife died and moved to California to marry another woman.

Fortunately books became a way for me to make some sense of these powerful and often fearful stories. My second grade teacher told my mother I was falling behind in reading. The teacher recommended we go to the library to get books to interest me. Not being a reader herself, Mom had the librarian select books. Luckily, those first books were juicy fairy tales not yet prettified by Disney. I loved them. A wicked stepmother who got thrown into an abyss, the witch tossed into an oven, the wolf almost devouring Little Red Riding Hood. What delicious violence. Grimm led to other books.

So my devotion to the library started then. Soon I was reading way ahead of my grade level. Feisty Nancy Drew was an inspiration along with the Hardy boys. I loved *Heidi, Black Beauty, The Swiss Family Robinson.* Soon I was moving on to more adult books. Though my life was very circumscribed, reading took me on journeys. That started a lifelong love affair with books. That library, only a small storefront that smelled of musty books, became a haven far from the constrained walls of home.

Though I liked school, I hated Mondays! Besides the beginning of the school week, we Catholics at P.S. 60 had to line up and march out single file to take the trek to our religious instructions class. We had to walk the mile or so to All Saints School. I had to hold my little sister's hand and pray that the older boys would not fling ice balls at us during those long Buffalo winters. The harsh black-robed nuns did not welcome us and let us know we were one step from hell by attending public school. They were not shy about using their rulers to smack a leg or an arm or, their favorite, folded hands. Weekly we had to examine our conscience before the trip to the confessional. Any lingering sin hiding in a corner of our souls would mean damnation for sure.

Though my mother was mercurial and had an explosive temper, she was also funny and loving. At any family party, she was the center of attention. She would have a whole repertoire of sayings that made everyone laugh: "What's new? New York? New Jersey?" "I'd go out with Clark Gable if I was just six months younger." "Cary Grant could put his shoes under my bed!"

Mom had such a powerful role in our nuclear family, but her old school Italian parents had a huge impact on her. Grandma, who lived upstairs in our small, two-family home, was an invalid. Mom took care of her along with all the household tasks for both flats. What had severe repercussions for our family was that my mother's three older brothers assumed that she, the only daughter, would take care of their ailing mother. Sadly, my mother believed that, too.

The wooden houses on our one block street had been slapped together like stacked teeth, built for the workers at the nearby factories. One day when I arrived home from grammar school in about the seventh grade, our flat downstairs was quiet. No dinner started in the small kitchen overlooking the narrow driveway.

"Where's Mommy?" I shouted upstairs to Grandma's flat.

That was the day my feisty, tempestuous mother disappeared for several weeks. The hospital, I was told. But it felt as if she'd fallen off the map. The days in our two-bedroom flat were long without her. Only my younger sister and me. After Dad got home from work he would eat a hasty dinner and then disappear to the garage and work on various carpentry projects. He often had part-time jobs to supplement his factory job. Grandpa was gone, too, on his nightly tavern crawls. Often my sister and I would go upstairs and sit with Grandma, who was badly crippled. Though she tried to reassure us she did not know what happened to Mom.

When Mom returned, she was a shadow of herself. Her brain had been fried with an early form of shock treatment. She kept asking me "What day did I come back from the hospital?" or "When did we come home from visiting Aunt Isabelle?"

I tried very hard to reassure her, to support her fragile recovery. I became my mother's caretaker. Relapses seemed frequent over the next few months. Even years. She had fainting spells so often we kept smelling salts under the kitchen sink.

Mom told me later that the doctors wanted her to move away from the house we shared with my grandparents, that the strain of taking care of them as well as her own family was too much for her. But she seemed proud of the fact that she refused. "I need to take care of my sick mother." Since my grandfather was largely absent, she felt this profoundly. She did chafe in that role and resented her three older brothers, who did nothing to help out. However, she never did confront them. Perhaps it was easier to have fainting spells than to use her voice. This I would not understand until many years later.

Dad's family had a profound but different influence on me. We traveled frequently to my father's hometown of Westfield, sixty miles away. We stayed on my aunt and uncle's farm. There I could take walks in the woods and explore the barn with pigs, chickens, and cows. We helped harvest grapes and picked tomatoes and beans from the truck garden. Best were the strawberries and raspberries in the summer. I loved the farm, the freedom it gave me, and the peek into a different way of life.

Unlike the men in my mom's family and even my dad's brothers, Dad was easy-going and fun, never dictatorial with his family. Not only did we, his daughters, love that about him, but his extended family did as well. So when we visited the farm house, a steady stream of family would come to see Dad. He was the youngest of eleven. So many of his nephews and nieces were his age. They called him Uncle Phil, and clearly admired him. Often they would sit around the marble-topped kitchen table talking and drinking reheated coffee that sat on the gas stove all day.

Once when I was about thirteen, I convinced my sister to go with me into a wood far from the farm. I brought a pocket knife and marked the trees, as I had read in Zane Grey books, to make sure we would have a way back. But I was very wrong and paid for it. It was late October and hunters' shotguns surprised us. They echoed loudly, though we couldn't see them. We were terrified. When we tried to find our way back, we could not find the bread crumbs of my very rudimentary tree scratches. Eventually we found a way out and ran to the farm, never telling the family why we were so pale and anxious. My confidence in a sure path was shaken.

Back in the fifties I found my life circumscribed. But there were quotidian joys of neighborhood, friends, family. Everyone believed the future would be better. Since I was getting good grades in math, my father told me to study hard and maybe become an engineer. But I told him girls did not become engineers. I knew there were certain roles for women in the world.

At that time, our working class section of Buffalo felt like a small town. Our neighborhood had a thriving main street with many national chain stores like Grants and Woolworth. There were mom-and-pop stores, like Dehlinger's Meat Market, where my mom did her shopping; a local drugstore; and Nick the Greek's soda fountain with homemade ice cream and cherry Cokes that did not come in a bottle.

Summers meant great social gatherings. The adults would gather on each other's porch, drink beer, and chat. In the street, we kids played tag, kickball, even badminton, until the streetlights came on. Then the parents would call us to bed. Everyone seemed to be Catholic like our family, so the Church was central to us all. All the dads worked at the plants that dotted the Niagara River: Dunlop, Chevy, DuPont, and Bell Aircraft in Niagara Falls. All the moms stayed home, making house work and cooking an art.

In the fifties it seemed that all would stay the same with stable jobs and families. Years later, it began to collapse. Many of the industries left. Buffalo became a Rust Belt City with pockets of great poverty and a brain drain. While I was growing up I did not know that it would all change.

These early experiences shaped me. I did become a woman in the way of women in my family. I was raised a fifties girl shaped by my Italian American parents, the Catholic Church, and my working class neighborhood. They outlined a path, however, the map I got in youth did not work anymore. By chance and by choice, I had to find my own way.

Chapter 2
Linda: Education from Life

My Mama moved among the days
like a dream walker in a field
seemed like what she touched was hers
seemed like what touched her couldn't hold
she got us almost through the high grass
    —Lucille Clifton, *good woman:*
              poems and memoir

Mom sat across from me in our tiny kitchen. Scents from supper's fried potatoes with onions still lingered in the air. But the dishes had been washed and dried. The yellow Formica table wedged under the windows looked out on the narrow driveway into the house across from us. I think it was spring because I remember hearing kids playing a form of tag we called "Relievio" outside on our dead end street. I wanted to go outside. But I had a list of spelling words to memorize for a fourth-grade test. A list I did not want to engage in. Mom quizzed me and I missed some words over and over again.

My mother was an imposing woman. Almost five feet seven and what was called large-boned. Unfortunately, I took after my short father and his side of the family. When she raised herself up to her height and set her lips tight, I knew I was in for trouble. Unsure about the *i* and the *e,* I stumbled over "friend." I stumbled over a few more as well. My head was outside, listening to the shouts of the neighbor kids. What came next was a sharp slap. Then another. I began crying very loudly. Grandpa came downstairs and knocked on the door. He was the only one in the house who could challenge Mom when she was in that mood.

"Leave her alone. You're acting like a stepmother."

Mom was even more furious. "Go upstairs and mind your business. She's not going to be like me."

That incident has stayed with me. Partly because I never did learn to spell very well. Especially "friend." Or "neighbor." Or any of those other "*ie*" and "*ei*" words. And partly because Grandpa intervened for me. Nothing he had done before. Looking back, I think that Mom was embarrassed by her lack of education. She was forced to drop out in the beginning of tenth grade because Grandpa wouldn't buy her books. So she was determined that her daughters would not suffer her fate. Maybe my devotion to education came from her. That devotion took me on a path different from hers, and from those of the many unhappy women in our family.

Some years later I failed the entrance exam to Holy Angels Academy, a private religious girls' high school far from our home. Mom had that same glint in her eye as she pulled me onto the bus. She had on a new cotton housedress, not the faded one she wore at home with the ever-ready apron. We sat close to the front so we would not miss the stop for the transfer to the Hertel bus that would take me to this high school. Just the day before we had received a letter that said I failed the entrance exam. Mom held my eighth-grade report cards close to her ample belly. I knew that look on her face. I had seen it before.

Now that firm look told me she was not going to let a little exam stop me from getting an education at a fine private Catholic girls' school. At Holy Angels, we met with the principal in her sparse office with only pictures of saints on the wall. She sat behind her giant polished cherry desk, aloof in her starched black bonnet, her long black robes, with a giant, silver cross hanging around her chest. She looked at the report card, with all my high grades, and sniffed that those grades were from a public school, nowhere near as demanding as those from a Catholic school. I was intimidated but Mom did not give up.

"She had a bad cold the day of the entrance exam. I want her to have another try."

Mom pulled herself up to her full height in her seat. She held the principal's gaze. It was clear that Mom was not moving until she had what she wanted. The principal finally gave in. I was to come back the following day for a make-up exam, which I passed, but I wonder if the principal just wanted to avoid meeting Mom again.

That was the only time Mom came to my school until I graduated. On class day, she was sitting in the audience proudly watching while my name was announced as only one of two Regents scholarship winners. I was proud, too. I never really felt at home at that school. But on that day, I felt like our family had been vindicated. Back when I had selected this school among several possible girls' high schools, I did not understand that the girls who attended were from middle and upper class backgrounds. There were only a handful of working class girls like me with blue collar dads and limited financial resources. It would be years before I realized that it was the class differences that had made my time there uncomfortable.

The education I received at Holy Angels had a profound impact on me all my life. The Catholic religious training was stringent. In addition, the Grey Nuns who taught us had almost a medieval view of how young women should behave. We had to march along the halls in silent single files. Our uniforms were ugly brown jumpers with yellow blouses. Our Buster Brown oxford shoes were appalling. They were the type of laced shoes our grandmothers wore. Whenever a nun entered a classroom, we were required to jump up and stand at attention. During Lent, we reflected on the sufferings of Jesus on the cross in detail. Sister Marie would recount his fever, his flayed flesh, his feet broken by nails, his lanced side. All of which, she told us, were caused by our sins, both mortal and venial. My best friend and I discussed what kind of sin kissing a boy would be, should we be so lucky. Venial we decided. Of course doing anything more was mortal and hell fire would follow.

As was true for many of my Catholic school friends, the twin movements of Civil Rights and Vatican II indelibly marked my formative years. Beginning in the late fifties, I watched the African American protesters on television. In 1957, when I was a sophomore in high school, watching the brave students known as the

Little Rock Nine try to desegregate a school was life changing for me. Here were black young people close to my age trying to enter the Little Rock Central High School through a crowd of shouting angry white adults. There were few African Americans in my neighborhood. But the bravery of those young people far away instigated a concern for social justice, as it did for many of my generation.

Despite the fact that our families were not particularly interested in this issue, many of my friends and I saw the terrible forces African Americans faced right on our TV screens. I watched the Freedom Riders attacked by angry whites in 1961, the Birmingham Church bombing in 1963, the Selma to Montgomery March in 1965 as well as lots of other Civil Rights actions in between. I didn't know it then, but it would inspire how I would be as a teacher. But it would also cause conflict within my family. Maybe because my parents had so little themselves, they could not muster up much sympathy for African Americans or understanding of the pressures of racism. I am not sure. Later in life their attitudes changed.

In 1960, Pope John XXIII convened a Vatican Council to "open the windows of the Church and let in some fresh air." That was mind boggling to us Catholics raised on rules to be followed without question. The liturgy was changed from Latin to English. There was a new emphasis on reading and understanding the bible. Most exciting of all to me, having seen the treatment of African Americans as highlighted by the Civil Rights Movement, was the new emphasis on social justice. So much was going on elsewhere in the world as well. A young, handsome John Kennedy, who just happened to be Catholic, was elected president in 1960. His call to service in his inauguration speech resonated deeply: "Ask not what your country can do for you—ask what you can do for your country." A far cry from the words of politicians today!

There were Civil Rights actions led by Dr. Martin Luther King, Jr. It felt like the country was finally waking up to its racist past. The Catholic Church's new emphasis on social justice dovetailed with brave African Americans marching for voting and economic rights. Many priests and nuns joined in Civil Rights marches. It's hard to capture the ferment of the times. At the beginning of the sixties, it seemed as if the world would change, had to change, and as if nothing could stop it.

When I won a scholarship and could select a private college, I chose a local Catholic college for girls. Going away to school was not in the realm of possibility for my family. In D'Youville College I again encountered the very strict Grey Nuns. However, it turned out to be a good choice. I could live at home, which my family required for an unmarried daughter. The academics were demanding, and, best of all, I met a group of girls like myself from working class families. Waiting in the line at the bookstore to buy textbooks, I met Marguerite, who has become a lifelong friend. In my sophomore year, I met Mary, another lifelong friend. Later we were young mothers together who talked a great deal about ideas, books, current events, and parenting. Our husbands became friends as well. We raised our children together with vacations, picnics, dinners, and many discussions. We still do that.

Back in college, I also dated my high school sweetheart, the man with whom I have now spent over fifty years! Bob is inclined to be a family man, much like my dad. But I did interrogate him during our five years of dating. I wanted to be sure he was not prone to alcohol or violence, issues for some of the men in my family. On one of our first dates, he ordered root beer. So I thought that was a good sign. He did not seem like my authoritarian grandfather and uncles. I wanted to avoid that kind of man.

When Bob was away at college, we wrote letters. His were so appealing. When I hit bottom a couple of times, confessing to him that I felt I could not make it in college, he encouraged me to continue in my studies. He helped me stay on the path that would take me far from my mother's life.

In 1964, my senior year in college, I took the train to South Bend, Indiana, to meet Bob at Notre Dame for his senior dance. My mother was tearful as I left from the big drafty train station in Buffalo. I wondered why. I was only going to be gone for a few days.

The next day I found out what great life change approached. Bob and I took a walk in the lovely May weather to the Grotto on campus. Notre Dame is devoted to honoring the Holy Mother, Mary. On the campus was a stone grotto built to look like the grotto in Lourdes, France. There were banks of candles, flowers and inscriptions from those whose prayers had been answered. To committed Catholics raised in the fifties, Lourdes was a vital example of our faith. The campus at Notre Dame was and is the de facto capital of Catholicism in the United States. So the Grotto there had such significance for us. Perhaps young people today would not think it such an important place. But for us at the time it was sacred. As we knelt to pray, Bob presented me with an engagement ring. Obviously he had talked to my parents to tell them of our engagement before I left. I was surprised even though we had talked of marriage after college. I cried. We embraced. Then he went to his Saturday class, and I went to the library to finish my senior term paper. It kind of encapsulated our life as a couple, devoted Catholics and devoted students.

Chapter 3
Linda: Becoming a Teacher

Students can't be the only learners in a classroom.
Teachers have to learn, too.
　　　　　　　　　—Nancie Atwell, *In the Middle*

"Miss D, you better get out of the way," said the sweet looking ninth grade girl at East High School. "We have knives."

In the late sixties, Bob began teaching at a largely African American school, with a sprinkling of a few white students from the old Polish neighborhood. It was in an economically depressed section of the city. Since I was home with two babies, I was not teaching. Nor did I plan to teach. But both grandmas offered to watch the kids while I substitute taught two days a week. I was happy to substitute at Bob's school, East High School, not only for the extra cash, since Bob's salary was really stretched supporting us, but also because I wanted to get out of the house. No matter how delightful one's babies are, being homebound all day with two of them is not very stimulating. Or so it was for me.

One day when I was at East a large street gang surrounded the school. There were gang conflicts going on back then, but in those halcyon days only fists and knives were used. A gang leader was in the school, and the opposing gang was after him. Though it was the end of the day, we teachers were told not to dismiss the students. I guess it would be called a lockdown now. I was filling in for a home economics teacher. Then such classes were made up of only girls. Because the final bell had rung, and it was a hot June day, the girls wanted to leave. The old building retained the heat, so we were all sweaty and short-tempered. But there was that gang of boys outside the school, circling the building. Since it was so stuffy, I could not keep the girls away from the windows. Some of them knew the gang members outside and called to them from the open windows.

One of the girls said, "Miss Drajem, you have to dismiss us." They started for the door.

"No." I blocked their way, hoping I appeared strong.

They crowded around me; the room got hotter.

"Miss D, we have knives."

I knew they would not hurt me. Or so I hoped! They told me more for information and to show they could counteract the rough-looking boys outside.

"Why on earth do you have them?" I asked.

"Because, you just don't know what our neighborhood is like. We need protection."

I stood there for what seemed like forever. Finally, the police were outside dispersing the gang. The principal gave an all-clear to let everybody out. Whew! My blouse was heavy with sweat.

Years later, in 1975, I would return to this school as a full-time teacher of English. Deciding to return to full-time teaching was more anxiety-provoking than substituting. Unlike my mother, I found household tasks both boring and—well—work! It was not the intellectual work I liked, the reading and writing I enjoyed in college and my first two years of teaching. Though I missed the challenge of using my B.A. in English after my boys were born, I knew that full-time women workers neglected their children, their homes, their husbands. At least that is what I had been told by my mother, my church, and even the media.

However, Bob and I had purchased a bigger house and just his paycheck wasn't covering all the bills. We thought it important to send our children to private Catholic elementary school. In addition, we wanted to be able to travel with our kids and give them some experiences we never had. Both sets of our parents struggled financially when we were young.

Secretly, I was glad that I had an economic reason for going back to work. That took away some of the guilt of becoming a working mother. Of course I loved being a mother, but staying home all the time was soul-killing for me. In Buffalo winters, since we did not have a second car, I was stuck home with my babies. Filling my time with housework, washing cloth diapers, and making dinners was not very fulfilling. I had good friends, like Mary and Marguerite. Since all of us were interested in books and current events we talked often on the phone, but both of them began working again before I did.

So when this full-time opportunity presented itself, I decided to take it. I selected East High School over other choices in the city of Buffalo because I knew there were many challenges there. By

1975, the school was made up of all African American students with mostly white teachers. It was still plagued by gang violence as well as poverty. Segregation had taken its toll. There were largely white schools and largely black schools. In 1976 the Federal Court ordered the Buffalo School District to come up with plans to work toward more racially diverse schools. But it would take many years for that to happen. The black schools were in neighborhoods suffering from rampant unemployment or underemployment. Often these schools were poorly funded by the largely white school board. Teaching for diversity was not on the horizon, so experienced teachers often opted for the white schools. In some small way, I felt I was bringing whatever abilities I had to assist a school with many problems.

Many years later, I would learn that cultural expectations shaped educational experiences. I would learn that race and social class can have a powerful impact on students, especially when their lives are far different from their teachers' lives. But, at that time, I knew I wanted to know my students and I wanted to teach them. That just seemed like common sense. Find out where the students are and try to teach them the skills they will need to navigate the wider society.

The school was chaotic, maybe in part because students did not see their needs being met. The fire alarms required by New York State sent kids home for the day. A trip to the lavatory often meant a student returned smelling of pot. Many students only attended school sporadically. So it was difficult for me to keep some momentum in lessons from day to day. But then a new principal came to the school, William Bennett. He was an African American man who had taught at the school for years, so he really knew the students. He created a new learning environment. His firm demeanor established rules that prevented smoking pot on campus and unruly behavior in class. It did not change things overnight, but the more egregious behaviors were eliminated.

My classroom was a converted closet crammed with desks. Trying to make it as attractive as possible, I spruced it up with posters, pictures of flowers, seashores, and inspiring quotes. I went to secondhand stores to get paperback books to build up a classroom library. The school board did not see fit to make sure the school was equipped, so I tried to supplement as best I could. I made dictionaries and textbooks available by borrowing from friends at other schools.

My college education classes had not in the least prepared me to teach these students. In those long-ago days, preparation was for a classical education aimed at middle-class students who knew they were college bound. Actually, for middle-class white students. When I ran into the nun who taught me literature at D'Youville, I told her I was teaching at this school.

"Well, they need to be taught." She sniffed and walked away.

I thought teaching was lecturing but that clearly did not work. Nor did teaching Latin origins of English words. Or reading Thoreau and Hawthorne. Often kids either ignored me or argued with me and called me a few names. Each night I went home and cried because I did not know what to do. But another teacher gave me some advice. He said, "Try a brief essay that can be read in one class period and then have student discuss it and write about it. You never know if they will be back the next day."

So, to engage the students, I tried introducing some short essays with debate-worthy topics. One day, in response to the assigned essay, I divided the class into two groups and asked one to argue for and one to argue against the topic of the essay, discrimination against women. What a surprise when students got so excited about something they read. They began debating loudly. My goal was to get them to write persuasive essays on the topic. But I did not anticipate that they would get so enthusiastic. Or loud! At the highest pitch of the debate, Principal Bennett walked in. A former college basketball player with an athletic build, he was an imposing tall man of confident demeanor.

I was embarrassed. Keeping students calm and under control was important in our urban school system. Teachers were evaluated on their ability to do that. So were principals. In other city high schools, principals who were considered successful ran their schools with military precision and stringent control. Not much attention was given to the actual learning going on. Consequently, I was concerned that the new principal would think I was not doing my job. He asked me to see him after school.

Rather nervously I walked into his office. I stuttered as I explained what we were doing, and what my goals were for the lesson.

"I see. A good plan. At least the students were debating an issue, which means they were thinking. Don't worry about it."

He was a no-nonsense kind of guy, and his affirmation seemed sincere. I was impressed because I knew principals had transferred or fired teachers for less. Mr. Bennett had my undying admiration after that.

The students did write essays, albeit brief and with lots of grammatical errors, but it was fine with me because they were writing. I learned something about how to engage students. Another colleague was a great proponent of what we called in educational jargon 'free writing.' And I became a believer as well. Free writing encouraged writing without judgment on the teacher's part so students could tell their own stories. They wrote about their lives, which were very different from my experiences growing up in a blue collar neighborhood. I did not encounter the violence that many of my students endured in this part of the city. I learned more than I anticipated. And students learned that teachers could appreciate them for who they are. It was an education for us all. Of course, that kind of writing did not fit in with the five-paragraph essay so endeared to English curricula. But letting them write about their personal experiences produced writers who could explore the difficult choices they saw in their lives. At least that was my hope.

In the spring of 1977, a professor from the University of Buffalo offered an on-site course on African American authors. Because I realized my students needed to read books by authors who looked like them, I eagerly signed up. I discovered Richard Wright and James Baldwin among other authors of color not included in my college English curriculum. When I shared some selections from these authors with my students, they responded eagerly. I loved having them read the portion of Frederick Douglass' autobiography in which he tells how he tricked a white boy into teaching him to read. I wanted my students to see how important literacy was and is.

My students taught me a great deal. They taught me that there is no one way to teach or to learn, that a classical education might be right for some but not all. They taught me that educators need to look closely at their students and learn from them. My students were not the middle-class students imagined by my college education classes. They came from single parent homes where poverty caused parents to work several minimum-wage jobs. So there was little supervision. Other families were broken by the stresses of alcoholism or drug use. There were gang members in my classes who sold drugs and saw no advantage to education. There were hard-working students who wanted to go on to college and did.

But I really loved my students. After they harassed me during the first semester, they became more cooperative in the second. It seemed to me that they were testing me. One day while I was on cafeteria duty, a student from another class refused to follow the rules and return her tray to the proper station. When I tried to remind her to do so, she became belligerent, which unfortunately was not unusual. Then I heard one of my students say to her, "Leave Miss D alone. She is my teacher."

I felt great. Now I had become a real teacher!

Chapter 4
Christopher: Different

Nothing I did or said among the other boys came to me naturally. As a result, in every encounter, even the most glancing, I had to be a performer, for at all times I was aware I was impersonating a human being.
—Edmund White, *A Boy's Own Story*

When I was in preschool, I got married to a girl in my class. My friend Eddie was the minister. He lived around the corner, and, walking to school, we would sometimes sing "Bad, Bad Leroy Brown" at the top of our five-year-old lungs, horrifying Mom when we got to the line that said *damn*.

Who was the girl I married? I don't remember. Why the marriage ceremony? I don't think it was a crush. At least not a crush on her. I did not know in 1973, at the age of five, that I was gay, but I did have a sense that I was different. I wasn't all that interested in going outside with Eddie and the other boys to play ball at recess. The impending nuptials gave me an excuse to stay inside with the bride-to-be and discuss the dress, make tissue-paper flowers, and decorate the classroom for the ceremony. I was crushing on the idea of all that beauty.

Our large, four-bedroom home on Parkside Avenue was in the white, distinctly middle-class neighborhood of North Buffalo. My parents were both high school teachers. Our neighbors were not only teachers like them, but also professional dads and stay-at-home moms, some nurses, and, on the streets farther away from the railroad tracks, a few lawyers and judges. Our house, brick on the front, had been painted a deep red on the sides and back by the previous owner, and Mom and Dad kept it that shade until they sold it. By contrast, the more upscale neighbors had houses painted in muted tones of moss or slate blue, and the only touch of red was the front door and the potted geraniums.

I knew just about all of the kids in the neighborhood. Together with my brother, Mark, who is just a year older than me, I spent warm summer nights playing tag in the streets or riding a bike in the church parking lot at St. Rose of Lima Catholic Church half a block from our house. Everyone we knew was Catholic, and all the children attended St. Rose. There was a Jewish synagogue only a few blocks away, and each Saturday several men and boys in their yarmulkes and women and girls in somber dresses marched off to temple. We never met those kids.

In an uninspired, patrician voice that strained at friendliness and compassion, Fr. Francis Edmeston intoned from the pulpit each Sunday. Starting in fourth grade, I joined Mark in serving Mass at St. Rose. Arriving at church a half hour before the service, we donned our long, white cassocks, lit some candles, and set out the wafers, water, and wine that we would deliver to the priest during the service. Looming over the altar was Christ on the cross, head pierced by a crown of thorns, side gashed by a spear, the downcast glance not accusing but full in equal parts of sorrow and warning. The readings early in the Mass might be a reminder of the power of love from one of the prophets or something from one of the Gospels such as Jesus reminding us that, as sinners, we were not to cast the first stone.

But it was the second part of the Mass that dealt the biggest punch. The priest consecrated the tasteless wafers that became, magically, the body of Christ; the water and the wine, His blood. I ate the wafers, sipped a bit of wine, and left there knowing that this guy—God's only son!—had died for me. I didn't need another glimpse of the look on the face of the suffering Jesus Christ to remember that I was not to mess up that week. I knew full well that the message would be delivered with equal drama again next Sunday.

Mark and I attended school next door to the church, learning to read and do math and memorize our commandments. We were also busy preparing for the sacraments, a series of seven lifelong rituals meant to be embraced as the sign of God's grace in our lives. With each sacrament, we would nourish, strengthen, and give expression to our faith. At least that's what the priests and nuns at school told us. The sacraments were determined by our age, and there was no choice of whether or not we would accept them. By virtue of being born into a Catholic family in the middle part of the twentieth century, we listened to what our parents told us to do and followed the plan. If we didn't, Dad would yell, and we might get hit with a really strong hairbrush that my parents still use to this day to brush their hair. I'm also pretty sure that Mark and I looked forward to each new sacrament because, after the religious celebration in church, there was always a party, and our grandparents and aunts and uncles gave us cards with five or ten dollars in them.

Baptism was the first sacrament, and it usually happened soon after birth. I was baptized in a pure white, delicately embroidered dress, worn by Mom, my aunt, and Mark before me as well as by my cousin Lillian years later. For each of us, with parents and godparents gathered around, holy water was poured over our heads, and our lives in the mercy and love of God and Jesus Christ began.

The second sacrament we received was penance, when we were expected to confess our sins to Fr. Edmeston and by doing so seek forgiveness. It was when we were in second grade that the mystery of the confessional booth was revealed. Pitch black and no bigger than a closet, it was located at the back of the nave in St. Rose. After the door swung closed and blocked out all the light, you knelt down near a wooden screen and waited. There was a booth on each side of the priest's cubicle, so sometimes we had to sit in the dark and wait while the other penitent was confessing their sins. You were not supposed to be listening, but there wasn't much to distract you while you were kneeling there in the dark, and one time I heard a classmate confess that he had farted in his little brother's face. I was appalled.

Fr. Edmeston somehow knew you were there, and he slid the screen open so that you could talk to him. Because it was dark and he was old and wore glasses, he couldn't really see you. The opening of the screen was our cue to begin with the memorized script: "Bless me, Father, for I have sinned. This is my first confession." There followed the litany of horrendous sins: uneaten green vegetables, not saying please and thank you to my parents, calling my brother stupid. The exact details escape me, but, looking back, I cannot imagine what sins I had committed at age seven.

After confessing my sins, I was expected to say an act of contrition: "O my God, I am heartily sorry for having offended you, and I detest all my sins because I dread the loss of heaven and the pains of hell, but most of all because they have offended you, my God, who are all good and deserving of all my love. I firmly resolve, with the help of your grace, to confess my sins, to do penance, and to amend my life. Amen."

It was a lot to remember for a seven-year-old, and frightening. Would I really risk losing out on an eternity in heaven simply for talking back to Mom? Would the burning flames of hell lick my delicate skin forever if I called Mark stupid? Fr. Edmeston's monotonous response to our act of contrition was shorter: "I absolve you from your sins in the name of the Father, and of the Son, and of the Holy Spirit." Then he gave us our penance, which meant returning to the pew, kneeling again, and silently saying three Hail Marys and two Our Fathers, or whatever else we were told. With images of pearly gates and the horns of the devil in mind, I knew enough to not take any chances. I said those prayers. Every single word.

That was my first of many acts of penance. Then there was the party with all our relatives and the cards with money.

I adored my first-grade teacher, Sister Rosalie, a slight, short-haired woman who played the guitar at the folk Mass each Sunday and sang about how they would know we were Christians by our love and that we should be not afraid because Jesus goes before us always. She was strict for sure, but in a kind and loving way. I wanted to hug her and make her smile because she had a great smile. I wanted to please her maybe more than I wanted to please my parents. When she awarded me the "Math Whiz of Grade 1" certificate at the school assembly in June, I beamed.

Mrs. Hamilton was my second-grade teacher, and she was the exact opposite of Sr. Rosalie. Older, prim, and starchy, Mrs. Hamilton didn't sing at the folk Mass, but rather in the church choir at the formal Mass on Sundays at noon. I could pick out her clear, sanctimonious voice above the wheezing grandeur of the organ in the loft at the back of the church.

Mrs. Hamilton scared me. She drew straight lines on the blackboard with a five-pronged wire tool that held pure white chalk and resembled a medieval torture device. On those lines, she taught us how to write neatly in cursive, both lowercase and uppercase letters, over and over again. It was also during second grade that we moved on in math from addition and subtraction to multiplication, and we were also expected to write out our times tables until they were burned into our memory. Whenever our class was noisy, Mrs. Hamilton would turn out the lights in the classroom and make us put our heads down on our desks and be quiet. It was often dark in the room. Slowly we would begin to hear the sounds of the world around us: snow blowing against the drafty windows in the winter or birds and neighborhood dogs barking when the windows were open in the spring. The most depressing sound was the sound of laughter leaking through the walls from Sr. Rosalie's classroom next door.

My older brother Mark was the athletic, smart, and popular one in the family. During the summers, he played Little League baseball. I played for two or three years, starting when I was eight years old, but spent most of the time staring into the clouds, fretting over getting grass stains on my uniform, and praying to sweet Jesus, the Blessed Virgin Mary, and the company of saints that nobody hit a pop fly to left field.

In school, I earned good grades, mostly because I worked hard. On the first day of school each year, I was asked, "Are you Mark's brother?" The teachers nodded after my affirmation, and it was clear to me that they would Expect Big Things. I constantly felt that I never delivered, but that if I worked harder, paid more attention to detail, and did not bother them or other students, I could succeed.

If I was lucky when I walked home after school, Mom wouldn't be home yet from work and I could go next door and watch cartoons with Dan, Mary, and Mike. If Mom was home, I would put my John Denver record on the stereo, plug in the headphones with the twenty-foot, curly cord, and lounge on the couch listening to "Sunshine on My Shoulders" while reading *Highlights* magazine and ignoring the actual sunshine outside.

In the pages of *Highlights,* I found additional reminders of expected behavior. There in each issue was a cartoon of Goofus and Gallant, another pair of what I imagined were brothers, the right and good Gallant and his rude and disrespectful brother Goofus. "Goofus bosses his friends. Gallant asks: 'What do you want to do next?'" Well, of course Gallant does, I thought. That's only polite. Who wouldn't do that? Who *is* this Goofus? "Goofus turns on the television when there are guests; whenever guests arrive, Gallant turns off the television at once." Yes, Gallant, good work. No penance needed for him.

In the winter, under Dad's supervision, Mark and I worked with Mike and Dan to turn our backyard into an ice rink. All but a thin layer of snow would be shoveled away and piled into a ring around the perimeter of our adjoining yards. Then Dad would spray the yard with layer after layer of water until it iced over into our own private rink. My grandfather built two hockey goals out of plywood and chicken wire, and we pulled out the barrel of hockey sticks from the back of the garden shed.

As a kid growing in up Buffalo, I was pretty much required to own skates, but I refused to follow Mark this time and play hockey. Because I refused even to own a pair of hockey skates, Dad relented and bought me a pair of sleek black figure skates that I came to treasure. I liked to play freeze tag on the rink, or the game where we would skate as fast as we could and leap over the bank at the rink's edge, each of us trying to jump higher or in a more spectacular way than the boy before us. Invariably Mark and his friends wanted to play hockey. I could tough it out for a game or two, but their checking and slashing often left me in tears. As I headed inside, I would yell, "You are so stupid! I will never play with you again!" Another trip to the confessional was in the cards for me, but I didn't care.

Mom, on duty in the kitchen, would welcome me in and offer me hot cocoa, and I would line up my hat and gloves on the kitchen floor in front of the furnace register so they could dry out. I would find the latest Hardy Boys book I was reading and sulk under an afghan blanket on the couch in the family room. After a while, I might drag myself over to the upright piano in the corner and practice my scales and plunk through Bach's Minuet in G Major, a song I was expected to play at the annual recital.

Music became my thing. Mark had hockey and baseball, and I became the family musician. Each week for a period of several years, Frank, a young music teacher who taught with my dad, came to our house and tried to instruct me in the ways of proper finger placement and chord progressions. Mom loved the fact that the extended family could gather around the piano at Christmas and sing carols, even though, while I played, everyone struggled to keep time with my missed notes and odd syncopation.

My paternal grandparents took me to see Liberace perform as he toured through Buffalo. The concert was at a place called Melody Fair, a theater in the round with a stage that slowly rotated throughout the performance. The crowd oohed and ahhed at Mr. Showmanship's outrageous costumes of ostrich plumes, rhinestones, and, of course, many, many rings. At one point, he strolled on stage in a powder-blue suit, ruffled jabot at the neck, and a long cape tied at the neck with a bow that ended in two large fur balls. Dangling them over a woman in the front row, Liberace teased, "Do you want to squeeze my balls?" The crowd of blue hairs loved it. Grandpa sucked his teeth in disapproval, but I could hear Gram chuckling under her breath.

Early in Liberace's career, when he traveled to Europe for a tour in the summer of 1956, the *Daily Mirror*, a British tabloid, reported that "[t]hey all say that this deadly, winking, sniggering, snuggling, chromium-plated, scent-impregnated, luminous, quivering, giggling, fruit-flavoured, mincing, ice-covered heap of mother love has had the biggest reception and impact on London since Charlie Chaplin arrived at the same station, Waterloo, on September 12, 1921." Liberace sued the paper for libel, claiming that the phrase "fruit-flavoured" hinted that he was homosexual, a claim he denied publicly until his death of AIDS-related complications in 1987. Liberace won the case and told reporters that he "cried all the way to the bank."

Liberace's fans willingly went along with the charade, happy to overlook his over-the-top persona because he was a great performer who provided all the spectacle necessary to distract them from the recessionary economy of the mid-1970s. After the performance, we attended a dinner hosted at a nearby restaurant owned by friends of my grandparents, and Liberace himself was the guest of honor. There's a photo of a young, gap-toothed me dressed in a brown plaid leisure suit and a white collared shirt. I am sitting on Lee's knee, as his perfectly coifed pompadour gleams black and that twinkling, mischievous smile plays to the camera.

No men that I knew would be caught dead wearing anything remotely similar to the costumes worn on stage that night. Dad's starched and pressed work shirts were neatly arranged in my parents' walk-in closet next to his collection of ties, wide and striped, waiting on a special hanger to be chosen as part of his daily work outfit. In Dad's bureau, there was one whole drawer full of what seemed like dozens and dozens of black and brown knee socks and another drawer full of Fruit of the Loom undershorts and crew-neck undershirts.

The walk-in closet in Mom and Dad's room housed a stairway to the attic. We had to carry Christmas decorations down from the attic in winter and store our snowsuits, hats, and gloves up there in the summer. The closet became a hideaway for me when I was trying to avoid playing hockey or practicing the piano. If I knew Mom was busy downstairs, I tiptoed into her and Dad's room, opened the door to the closet, and perched on the raised step that led to the narrow door to the attic.

Across the closet was Mom's side, with its collection of skirts, suits, and polyester blouses that made up her professional uniform. Under plastic dry-cleaning bags were fringed shawls and colorful cocktail dresses. A hatbox underneath the sewing basket held a wiglet she had worn in the early 1970s. A cloth-lined jewelry box contained a trove of brooches that I recognized from sepia-toned photos of my great-grandmother. On occasion, I might hold one up to myself in front of the dresser mirror and stare back at my reflection.

Outside the house, smokestacks from Bethlehem Steel belched the last of their rust-belt gloom, and the warm days of March left piles of blackened snow. Inside that closet, clothes and jewelry and scarves shone brightly in the filtered light, full of forbidden style and grace. Displayed on a shoe rack as if they were works of art were the pristine white satin shoes that my mother wore on her wedding day, the navy heels she wore to work, and a pair of sandals with thick cork soles.

Not content to just view these treasures, I decided one day to remove a silky scarf from a hanger and gracefully wrap it around my neck as I had seen Mom do so quickly while hurrying out the door to work. Carefully, I removed a pair of shoes from their slot and slipped them on. Sticking to the carpeted area so that no one would hear, I somehow missed the telltale click of the basement door and the creak of Mom's footsteps coming upstairs. Either sound would have given me enough time to quickly slip off the shoes, tuck them and the scarf away, and duck out of the closet, but I missed my chance.

The towering pile of laundry in the basket Mom carried with her when she entered her room was not enough to hide the fact that there I stood in front of the mirror, wearing the patent leather pumps and the paisley scarf.

"What are you doing?" she asked, a rare look of anger and betrayal on her face.

"Uh...nothing?" I stammered as I kicked off the shoes, flung the scarf, and fled the room.

I put as much distance as possible between Mom and me for the rest of the day. She graded papers at the kitchen table, and I reorganized the desk drawers in my bedroom. Later in the afternoon, she and Dad had an argument about something else, and I listened from the family room, scanning *Boys' Life* and tallying who was winning.

Despite the stacks of essays, mounds of laundry, and meals to prepare, Mom would always drop everything that she was doing and focus her attention on us when we needed something. Her reservoirs of patience and attention seemed endless.

That day was one of the rare occasions when that wasn't true. At one point, Mom stormed upstairs, laundry basket in hand, ready to fold and put away another load.

"I've got a husband who won't help me with the laundry and a son who wears women's shoes!"

There was such disappointment in those words. I would have done almost anything to get back into Mom's good graces. I made a commitment to stay out of her closet and to redouble my efforts to be good at being a boy. I didn't need the dark confessional or the prompting of Fr. Edmeston. That night in bed, alone in the silence, I mumbled two Hail Marys and an Our Father, closed my eyes, and went to sleep.

Chapter 5
Christopher: Sin

Everyone, man and woman, should acknowledge and accept his sexual identity. Physical, moral, and spiritual difference and complementarity are oriented toward the goods of marriage and the flourishing of family life. The harmony of the couple and of society depends in part on the way in which the complementarity, needs, and mutual support between the sexes are lived out.

Catechism of The Catholic Church, Part Three: Life in Christ
Section Two: The Ten Commandments
Chapter Two: "You Shall Love Your Neighbor as Yourself"
Article 6: The Sixth Commandment—
You Shall Not Commit Adultery
Section 2333

Just four blocks from my childhood home stood the Discalced Carmelite Monastery of Buffalo, New York. This was the home of a group of Catholic nuns, young women who had given up reading newspapers, watching television, and dating to work in the monastery garden, attend Mass in the soaring chapel, and silently marry themselves to Jesus Christ.

From the ages of ten to fourteen, I served Mass along with

Mark at the monastery chapel. We were expected to commit to a week of Masses at a time, and I hated getting up at six o'clock in the morning for five days straight knowing that nothing but a long day at school would follow. Looking back now, my concerns seem petty and small compared to a life of silence, sandals, and a husband who had been dead for almost two thousand years. When we arrived at the side door, an external nun greeted us; we affectionately called them "outies" and the cloistered nuns "innies." The outies could talk to regular people like us, and they served the monastery as a link to the outside world, doing the shopping, driving innies to doctor's appointments, and often doing yard work on the grounds outside the high brick walls that enclosed the innies' gardens.

Mark and I were the same height and looked alike, so we helped to create a good stage picture on the altar. We were therefore a hot commodity for special occasions such as Christmas Eve Midnight Mass and the rare but elaborate investiture ceremony. In the latter, a new Bride of Christ, her head adorned in a full veil framing clear skin and rosy cheeks, and wearing a long, mud-brown habit, took her vows in front of a packed chapel of family and community members. The vows were taken during an extra-long Mass presided over by the bishop. At the beginning of Mass, Mark and I could spy the full contingent of nuns sequestered to the right of the altar behind a large, black wire screen that was revealed when the outie drew a deep red curtain. At the end of the investiture, we dutifully followed the bishop to a small room at the back of the nave where we were granted a short audience with the new innie. "Don't do it!" I wanted to shout. "You will never be able to see another episode of *The Love Boat* or dance to Michael Jackson's 'Don't Stop Till You Get Enough'!'"

The Ten Commandments are great rules to live by, and my religious education at school and home certainly taught me right from wrong. Mom and Dad were brought up in the church of the Latin Mass and according to a strict catechism, which was basically the rulebook for all Good Catholics. As parents, they focused much more on the spirit of the law as opposed to the letter of it, placing God's commandments in a social context. For them, Jesus was an agent of social change who was concerned about the less fortunate and those who were broken and in need. The story of Jesus getting angry with the moneychangers in the temple had practical application during the excesses of the Reagan Republicans in the 1980s. In my family, and in the community of friends and neighbors that we spent time with, the adults were giving, caring, and full of what I knew to be the best of the Catholic faith I was raised in.

But rules are rules, and the rules of Catholicism were clear: homosexuality is a sin. The Old Testament states in Leviticus 20:13 that "If a man also lie with mankind, as he lieth with a woman, both of them have committed an abomination: they shall surely be put to death; their blood shall be upon them." The message is reinforced in the New Testament's 1 Corinthians 6:9-10: "Know ye not that the unrighteous shall not inherit the kingdom of God? Be not deceived: neither fornicators, nor idolaters, nor adulterers, nor effeminate, nor abusers of themselves with mankind, [n]or thieves, nor covetous, nor drunkards, nor revilers, nor extortioners, shall inherit the kingdom of God."

These passages created the foundation for a modern interpretation of God's disdain for homosexuals. Never mind that scholars have repeatedly called into question the original meaning and intent of these passages, or that Christians are selective in our modern world about the biblical passages they choose to follow. Shellfish, anyone? Mixed-fiber clothing? Tattoos? All, according to Leviticus, are an abomination.

It is biblical passages like these, in fact, along with outdated stereotypes, misinformation, and lack of understanding, that have led to the development of the Church's position on homosexuality. As laid out in the catechism, in language that still exists to this day, homosexual behavior is described as a sin:

> *Basing itself on Sacred Scripture, which presents homosexual acts as acts of grave depravity, tradition has always declared that 'homosexual acts are intrinsically disordered'. They are contrary to the natural law. They close the sexual act to the gift of life. They do not proceed from a genuine affective and sexual complementarity. Under no circumstances can they be approved.*

The message to good Catholics attracted to members of the same sex is clear: You are disordered. Deny your natural urges. Repent of any unclean thoughts. Your pain and struggle are insignificant compared with that of Jesus Christ. He died for your sins. Remember? God will punish you if you do not change these thoughts and desires. Pray for change.

By the time I was in fifth grade, I did want to change. Let me be clear: at age ten I wasn't identifying as gay, but I did know that I was different. I didn't have the awareness or the words to articulate the nature of my difference, but I found that I just didn't fit in with the other boys. When we lined up in the parking lot outside school in the morning and at lunch, when we were in gym class playing dodgeball with Sr. Ruth, when we sat in the library for one of Fr. Edmeston's lessons about the Bible, I always felt like a stranger in a strange land. The boys seemed to have a language all their own, a set of jokes that made sense only to them, a way of shutting me out because I wasn't like them. In fact, I was increasingly becoming a target.

"You going to play cat's cradle with the *girls?*" they whispered.

"Chrissy is a sissy," they taunted.

"Chris and Brian sitting in a tree, K-I-S-S-I-N-G..." they sang.

Mom and Dad noticed that something was not quite right and decided that perhaps a change of schools would be good. Every day, starting in sixth grade, I took a school bus across the city to Campus East, a magnet school that drew students from all over Buffalo as part of an effort to desegregate city schools. The forty-five-minute bus ride carried me from the area of the city I knew so well through neighborhoods I had never seen before. The scenery was different, the school was different, and, for the first time in my life, I was attending school with non-Catholic and African American students.

For some time after I started, I was filled with a sense of fear that once again I would find myself shut out and that the boys riding in the last few seats on the bus would discover that I was different. I sat up front, close to the driver and the bus aide, and stared out the window as the bus made its way past St. Rose, the Carmelite monastery, and through North Buffalo to the East Side. It didn't take long for the scent of my fear to drift to the boys on the bus, and the name-calling and taunting began.

For many who suffer through constant verbal abuse, it's difficult to recall a specific incident. Did they call me a faggot? Did they lisp and swish and drop their wrists? Throw spit wads? Undoubtedly. Did the bus driver or the aide intervene? Half-heartedly. "Boys will be boys," I now imagine them thinking to themselves. I know I was relieved when I got home. I know there was a tough shell that built up. I perfected my ability to ignore. To tune out. I also know that I developed a cynicism, a caustic and sarcastic sense of humor that was full of distrust and self-loathing and utter sadness.

In the gospel according to Luke, Jesus tells his apostles that he is going to suffer a lot and be rejected by those in positions of authority. He tells them that "[i]f any man will come after me, let him deny himself, and take up his cross daily, and follow me. For whosoever will save his life shall lose it: but whosoever will lose his life for my sake, the same shall save it." Passages such as this had a powerful impact on me. As I grew older, I denied myself by denying the impact of the teasing. Sure, it made me mad. Sure, it stung. But this was my personal cross to bear. And what was this in comparison to the suffering and death of our Lord and Savior?

Gym and swim class at Campus East were the worst. One day in gym class, I got pelted in the groin during a game of dodgeball.

The gym teacher, Mr. Sanders, seemed to find this as funny as the boys who had targeted me. He never seemed to be around in the locker room, where the state of undress provided an opportunity for my classmates to toss out jokes about how I might like to do any variety of things to them or want them to do things to me. Most of what they said was once again a foreign language to me. I had no idea what the terms meant that they tossed back and forth, and there was no internet back then on which to look it up.

A few times during sixth grade, the girls in our class were sent next door to the other sixth-grade class, and the boys from that class were sent to our room. Divided by gender, our sex education class began. It was here that the business of puberty was explained by Mr. Patterson, a balding, solemn man in his forties. Actually, Mr. Patterson didn't do a great deal of talking. Instead, he closed the shades, pulled down a screen at the front of the room, and showed a movie that told us that our voices would deepen, that hair would grow under our arms and that, when sexually aroused, our penises would become erect. Watching it all explained, seeing the diagrams, hearing the talk of testosterone and developed muscles, I felt as if I were being let in on a secret—scary and, yes, exciting. When the film was over, the lights came on and, because I was sitting closest to the windows, Mr. Patterson asked me to raise the shades. I hesitated. Prayed that I could make it quickly to the windows and back undetected. The barely-concealed laughter let me know my classmates had seen the bulge in my pants, and I knew I was in for even more taunts for weeks to come.

Those films in Mr. Patterson's class indicated that, during puberty, it was expected that we would develop an attraction to members of the opposite sex. This attraction was normal; it meant that we were becoming young men who could at some point choose to engage in sexual intercourse with a woman, impregnate her, and the result would be a baby. We were taught about birth control. We were taught about sexually transmitted diseases. Homosexuality was never mentioned.

Since I no longer attended Catholic school, Mom and Dad expected me to attend religious education classes at St. Rose after school. Each Wednesday, the few Catholic kids in the neighborhood who attended public schools were ushered into one of my old classrooms at St. Rose to attend Confraternity of Christian Doctrine classes, also known as CCD. The St. Rose students looked down on us; stolen pencils, gum on the bottom of desks, anything broken or misplaced was always blamed on the pubbies who attended CCD. I knew that because I had been part of the group shelling out the complaints when I was a student at St. Rose. Now I was one of them. A pubbie.

At CCD, we were given the religious perspective on puberty and sex. According to the catechism, "sexual pleasure is morally disordered when sought for itself, isolated from its procreative and unitive [between spouses] purposes." This one line covers a great deal. Contraception? Nope. Sexual acts need to lead to having kids. Even my limited public-school education taught me that a man and a woman were needed for that. Homosexual acts? Forget about it. Masturbation? Off limits as well, because sexual pleasure shouldn't be sought for itself. The catechism goes on to say that "[t] he deliberate use of the sexual faculty, for whatever reason, outside of marriage is essentially contrary to its purpose."

My older cousin Greg had a poster of Farrah Fawcett on his bedroom wall. She looked out, bright smile on her face, head titled back, blond hair cascading to her shoulders, nipples poking through her red one-piece swimsuit. My other cousin Dave was a fan of Bo Derek. On the wall in his bedroom was the poster from the movie *10* where she's jogging down the beach with her hair in braids and wearing a wet, flesh-colored bathing suit. One of the hit shows on television at the time was *The Dukes of Hazzard.* In her high-cut jean shorts and plaid shirt with the tails tied to reveal her navel, Catherine Bach as Daisy Duke was my best friend Joe Calamita's fantasy. I knew that she or Farrah or Bo were supposed to be mine as well.

The problem was that I wasn't attracted to Daisy in her short shorts. Farrah's come-hither smile wasn't doing it for me, either. Bo Derek in her braids and the see-through flesh-colored swimsuit was simply confusing. What's with the braids? It wasn't her but Bo *Duke*, played in all his blond-haired glory by John Schneider, who stirred things inside of me. I'm sure I was dreaming of him the night I woke up to find a strange substance in my pajamas and was convinced that God had punished me by breaking my penis.

I was also convinced that, along with the taunts and humiliation from my classmates, God was sending me a clear message: get yourself straightened out. The God of my youth was not a mystery. He was direct and clear. He knew everything and could see into the very depths of my soul. He knew things I could not even name.

It was through His grace, however, that I could find a way to tame these different thoughts, to not fall into a sinful trap.

First, my choice of reading material would have to change. No more JCPenney's catalogs, with their tempting pages of men in swimsuits and underwear. No more *Dynamite* or *Bananas,* which came with every Scholastic book order but too frequently had Shaun Cassidy or John Travolta on the cover. Mark's copies of *Sports Illustrated* became my new magazine of choice. I had found the text that would bring me salvation. With a devotion that rivaled that of the nuns in the monastery, and with the hope that some bit of sport detail would infect my vocabulary, I made my way through articles on college football and professional baseball. I would learn this foreign language if it killed me. When the annual swimsuit edition came in the mail, its photos of scantily clad women splayed out beside a pool or emerging from the surf of a tropical island, I staked out a prominent position in the family room to read it, thus proving to Mom, Dad, and Mark that I was interested. It escaped me that most teenage boys would much rather peruse that particular issue behind closed doors.

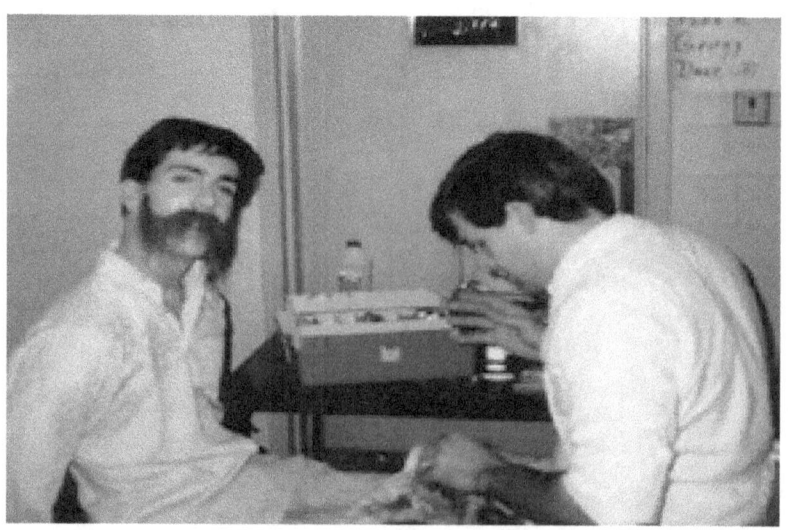

Chapter 6
Christopher: Fear

Fear and love cannot long remain in the same bed together....It's hard for a boy to find out who he is, or what he wants, if he is always afraid and always acting, and especially when his fear invades his most private life.
—James Baldwin, *Tell Me How Long the Train's Been Gone*

For a short period of time in high school, I wanted, more than anything, to be a Broadway star. When Mom and Dad took me to New York just before my sophomore year, we went to see *Cats*. A few weeks before the trip, my friend Todd and I were hanging out in my room after school, and he sang the highlights of the entire show to me. His clear, bright tenor, singing of Jellical cats and their memories, rang out throughout my house.

I was transfixed at first, then horrified by what was happening. I had never heard Mark and his friends singing lyrics from a Broadway musical, but here was Todd, flamboyantly full-voiced, belting out the highlights of song after song. And there could be no denying the sexual orientation of a young man who knew this recording by heart.

When we saw the show, I was mesmerized, just as Todd said I would be. I was convinced that I could be up there, singing, dancing, emoting. Now in high school, I was no longer a pubbie. Instead, I once again followed in my brother's footsteps and attended St. Joseph's Collegiate Institute, an all-boys Catholic high school. I spent my days basically trying to hide, doing everything I could not to stand out in any way, but I dreamed of putting on a costume of some kind, stepping into a role, and being up there, on the stage, all eyes on me. Never mind that I couldn't really carry a tune or dance. That didn't matter. I would learn. I would be a star.

In the fall of my sophomore year, I quit the swim team to become a thespian. I hit it big that year: I was cast as Bundles the laundryman in *Annie* at Mount St. Mary's, our sister school. Bundles does not have a big role, but it's a pivotal one; he's responsible for smuggling Annie out of the orphanage.

I must have proved my worth. The following year, I played Colonel Pickering, a secondary lead, in *My Fair Lady*. This was the big time. I was well on my way to making my dream of Broadway stardom a reality. Colonel Pickering is the friend of Henry Higgins, a phonetics professor who places a bet with Pickering that he can teach Eliza Doolittle, a poor flower seller, to speak proper English and pass her off as a duchess. Pickering actually has a big solo about midway through the show, singing about how Higgins did it, he managed to fool all his upper-crust friends into thinking that Eliza is, in fact, one of them.

On the day we were scheduled to rehearse my number, the entire cast was assembled around the piano in Mrs. Herman's choir room. The warm autumn sun was shining through the windows that were wide open to the campus just outside. As we ran through our vocal warm-up, I nervously checked and re-checked my sheet music. I was arranging it carefully on the black music stand in front of me when Mrs. Herman called me and the actor playing Henry over to the piano. My friend Sarah gave a quick smile and a wink, confirmation that I *had this*. I would sing my lines, Henry would sing his, and then the chorus would join in.

Mrs. Herman didn't so much play the piano as bang out the notes—a collection of them that at least resembled the notes in the score—and you got the sense of the piece. I did miss my cue the first time, however, and we started again. This time I had it. My voice, in all its sixteen-year-old glory, rang out through the room, out the open window, and spilled out across the campus. I was doing it. I was great.

Halfway through the opening verse, the piano abruptly stopped.

"Never mind," Mrs. Herman snapped. "The cast can sing your song."

I slunk back to my seat. Henry Higgins looked around, unsure what he was supposed to do. The chorus was taught my lines, which I was encouraged to mouth along with the rest. Sarah tried to console me after rehearsal, but she did have to say, "You sounded terrible."

There were straight jocks who were cast in the shows and, I was sure, there only to date girls. But it was clear that many of the other boys were, like me, different. Backstage and in the wings, there was a freedom to let go, to be overly dramatic and share gossip and same-sex crushes. I confided to Todd and Daniel, another backstage friend, that I was having certain feelings or that I was unsure about my sexuality. I never, however, uttered the words "I'm gay," even to my closest friends. I was convinced deep down it just couldn't be true. I followed the lead of the jocks and expressed my interest in girls. I dated first Colleen, then Tracy, then Lori, my high school sweetheart. This was proof to others that I wasn't gay, and it was an attempt to convince myself that perhaps those feelings about men would just go away.

In retrospect, it's hard to believe that my denial could be that strong and deep. I felt unsure of where I belonged. I wanted to be more like my brother and his friends. I yearned for the familiar and easy comfort of their joking and often intense intellectual debates. Although their conversation still often felt like a foreign language, the conversations backstage with Todd and Daniel felt foreign as well. I couldn't quote lines from old Bette Davis movies. I didn't know what it meant to be a friend of Dorothy, a reference to gay icon Judy Garland's character in *The Wizard of Oz*. I didn't feel comfortable or free channeling my inner drag queen, even backstage in the company of those I knew wouldn't care in the least and would have been glad to welcome me into the fold.

In 1983, the musical *La Cage aux Folles,* written by Harvey Fierstein, opened on Broadway. The story centers on two gay men, Georges and Albin, who share a life together as well as their work in a nightclub in Saint-Tropez where Albin is featured in a drag show. (The only reason I know this is because I saw the 1996 film

The Birdcage with Nathan Lane and Robin Williams, which was a remake of the 1978 Franco-Italian film *La Cage aux Folles*.)

It was when we were both acting in *Annie* that fall that Daniel introduced me to *La Cage*. At the most inopportune moments, when we were waiting in line at the convenience store across from school on our way to rehearsal, for example, he would start singing Albin's Act I finale "I Am What I Am".

Each time he broke into song, I was mortified. I never wanted to draw that much attention to myself offstage, and there's no better way to ensure that you are going to be called a faggot than singing the lines of a drag-queen performer from a musical about two queers. Or even being in the company of the person doing the singing. Looking back, I see that he was only trying to communicate to me that admitting I was gay, owning up to those feelings, would mean freedom, honesty, and authenticity. It was a message that I was not ready to hear.

That fall, Daniel kissed me one night during a sleepover after rehearsal. I couldn't get out of his house fast enough the next morning. I was filled with guilt and shame, terrified that somehow Mom and Dad would know what had happened the night before. On Monday, I was overcome by a new fear: what would Daniel say when I passed him in the hall? I was convinced that taunts of "faggot" and "queer" were delivered with a certain knowledge of what we had done over the weekend. I was desperate that something like that kiss would never, ever happen again.

Daniel was older than I and his locker was in the senior hallway. I avoided that hallway the following week so that I would see Daniel only at afternoon rehearsals. There we were at least out of the line of fire from seniors who claimed that prime territory between the main office and library on one end and the cafeteria on the other. I was used to avoiding the senior hallway and had a route I had carefully planned that would get me from Mr. Lennon's social studies class at the edge of the hall to Mrs. Heffern's religion class on the second floor quickly but without the chance of being bullied. Mark and his friends were in the halls, but so were the meat-headed senior bullies who liked to plow into underclassmen, taunting us in any way that made them feel fuller of themselves and surer of their masculinity.

Now I am older and a teacher myself. I know enough about adolescents to know that the insecurity and desire to fit in that leads young adults to cruelty is indiscriminate. I wish I had found a way to stand up for myself, to return their taunts, or to assert myself in some other way. At the time, I was filled with shame. I was convinced that I was wearing my difference, my secret desires, like a costume each day. The problem was that I didn't want anyone to notice this particular role. I wanted more than anything to blend in and be *normal* instead of being troubled each night by thoughts of the guy who sat behind me in homeroom.

The story of homosexuality in America in the 1980s is indistinguishable from the story of AIDS. On July 3, 1981, the *New York Times* printed the first story of a rare pneumonia and skin cancer found in forty-one gay men in New York and California. The Centers for Disease Control initially referred to the disease as GRID, Gay-Related Immune Deficiency Disorder. By the time I started high school in the fall of 1982, however, the National Gay Task Force had successfully lobbied to change the name of the disease to AIDS (Acquired Immunodeficiency Syndrome).

Daniel, Todd, and I whispered about the plague in the rare moments we had the presence of mind as teens to think about the world outside ourselves. President Ronald Reagan, who was silent about AIDS in the early days of the disease, finally said in 1985 that AIDS was a "top priority," but he didn't do enough to get direct funding for research and care. When attention in the media increased, it was covered as a mostly gay male problem. In those early days, before much was known about transmission and infection rates across the general public, unbiased, in-depth reporting was scarce.

Many fundamentalist Christians believed that the disease was God's punishment for those who engaged in homosexual behavior, a plague to kill off sinners. The Moral Majority's Rev. Jerry Falwell claimed that "AIDS is the wrath of God upon homosexuals."

Reagan's communications director Pat Buchanan argued that AIDS was "nature's revenge on gay men." Buchanan wrote in a 1983 op-ed for the *New York Post* that "the poor homosexuals—they have declared war upon nature, and now nature is exacting an awful retribution." He concluded that homosexuals should not be permitted to handle food and that the Democratic party's decision to hold their next convention in San Francisco would leave delegates' spouses and children at the mercy of "homosexuals who belong to a community that is a common carrier of dangerous, communicable and sometimes fatal diseases."

Many other religious leaders of the time didn't confine their condemnation to those who were HIV positive. Pat Robertson, a Southern Baptist minister and host of the popular Christian news and television show *The 700 Club*, used his pulpit to pedal the idea that God would seek retribution for society's acceptance of homosexuality through dangerous hurricanes, earthquakes, tornadoes, terrorist bombings, and even meteor strikes. James Dobson, an evangelical Christian leader, founded Focus on the Family in 1977, and began promoting the belief that homosexuality is a choice and not an inborn trait. Focus on the Family continues to support conversion therapy, the widely discredited idea that, through psychological or spiritual intervention, an individual can change their orientation from homosexual or bisexual to heterosexual.

When my parents had friends or family over for dinner, Mark and I now joined in the discussions about how Reagan's trickle-down theory of economics was a joke or how the Moral Majority was in fact neither moral nor a majority. But there was no outraged condemnation of the lack of funding for AIDS research. Nothing was said about the hate that emanated from the pulpits of evangelical preachers about gay men and women. In fact, there was relatively little discussion of anything having to do with gay people.

In part, this had to do with our religion. For Catholics, the official word from our church leaders on homosexuality was only slightly better than those in the evangelical community. Many historical church documents defined homosexual activity as *crimen pessimum*, the worst crime. Perhaps only slightly more comforting, Pope John Paul II clarified that homosexual activity was, as a willfully chosen activity, sinful behavior. He did allow, however, unlike Falwell and Buchanan and their ilk, that homosexual *orientation* was usually not a matter of free choice.

That was a distinction that was not addressed in the religious education I received at St. Joe's, and it wasn't something I even understood until I was much older. I was taught by the Christian Brothers and our lay teachers in religion classes that homosexuality was a sin, right along with abortion, birth control, and adultery. Any nuance that existed in the official message from the church was glossed over in my classes, along with the inherent absurdity of the position itself: *it's fine to be gay, but don't think about acting on those desires.*

When I was in high school, none of my parents' friends and none of our family members identified as gay. It felt to me as if gay people were a separate class of people. Some lived in Buffalo's Allentown neighborhood around Elmwood Avenue, but they kept to themselves and were not part of our world. If an adult mentioned a man who might be *that way,* the other adults snickered and shook their heads.

The lessons I learned from my parents and teachers while growing up—lessons also learned by those kids in the back of the bus in middle school and the halls of St. Joe's—not only identified homosexuality as a sin but also conflated sexual orientation and gender. Being a gay male was thought to be taking on effeminate qualities deliberately, being a sissy, and making a choice to reject everything strong, stoic, and masculine. A cultural belief still popular in the 1980s was that a son became gay because of an overbearing, dominant mother and an absent or disengaged father.

However, people believed it was the man himself who, consciously and deliberately, chose to forsake his own gender and instead chose to be more feminine.

My friend Todd was the rare gay young man who didn't give a crap what anyone thought of him and was willing to put his gay, effeminate behavior on display for all to see. Back in the 1980s, there weren't too many brave souls like him around, at least in Catholic, all-male private schools. Todd embraced his feminine side. For our senior-year winter formal, he wore a bright red sports jacket and a costume jewelry brooch, much to the chagrin of his date, our good friend Meghan. That spring, he played Teen Angel in our school's production of *Grease* and, in a fantasy sequence in Act II, sang "Beauty School Dropout" to Frenchy, encouraging her to return to high school after failing out of beauty school.

It was a role made for Todd. He brought the house down every night. I played Vince Fontaine, a radio disc jockey who emcees the school dance at which Danny, Sandy, and the rest do the hand jive. It was a role that suited me. I didn't have a solo to sing, and I was able to fake my way through the limited dancing I was asked to do. I also played a straight guy, albeit a rather creepy one since he tries to hook up with Marty, one of the Pink Ladies.

As seniors, Todd and I had certain privileges, and we would join the rest of our classmates at the diner down the block during our free periods, taking advantage of senior open campus to drink bottomless cups of coffee and eat fried eggs and toast. I worked on the school newspaper and the yearbook. After school, I attended play rehearsals and tried to study AP Calculus (after all, Mark had taken it and done well on the exam). In the evening, I filled out college applications and was the leader of the Catholic Youth Organization at St. Rose.

Everything I did that year was just playing a role, and the energy it took to play it was intense. Deep down I knew I was different, but I couldn't show anyone the real person. Every wardrobe choice, every sentence spoken in class, every mannerism needed to be carefully calibrated to project that I was the same, normal like everyone else.

Driving from the diner back to school one day, Todd told me about a store on Elmwood Avenue where they sold magazines of naked men. We drove over there after school. I was nervous about even being seen at this store in this neighborhood. Inside, there were bright white walls and, off to one side, the magazine racks. Sex and freedom and shame and guilt and blessed, sweet fascination. We looked around the store, examining this trinket or that, trying to be clear we were just browsing, when oh my, well, I just happened upon this magazine, goodness! Todd actually purchased one. I would never dare to bring such a thing into my home. Well, yes, maybe I would borrow it for a bit.

Mark had left home to attend college at Notre Dame, Our Lady's University, so during my senior year, it was just me and Mom and Dad. Without Mark around, it was too quiet. At some point during the year, Mom and Dad recognized that I was depressed. They asked if I wanted to go to see a therapist.

"We will all go together, at least at first," they said. "Then you can meet with him on your own, and we will meet with him separately. What you two discuss will be confidential."

It must have sounded all right at the time. I don't remember putting up a fight, and I suppose I was glad that they had recognized my sadness and depression and were looking for ways to help. Perhaps there was a way out of this. I was terrified that somehow they would find out about—or perhaps already knew?—the questions I faced about my sexual orientation. If Mom and Dad saw that I was depressed, perhaps they had seen more than that. There was a part of me that was relieved. Clearly, I was not able to find a way around these feelings. Perhaps this counseling would help me figure things out.

As we drove to each session, an uneasy silence settled between Mom and me in the car. I spilled my guts in the sessions, but I was determined to not give away more than was necessary to my parents. Lots of people were depressed. Only sinners, perverts, girly men, and outcasts were gay. I never let them in on what Dr. Roger and I discussed, and, although the possibility terrified me at the time, I had no reason to believe they knew anything of my closely guarded secrets.

Dr. Roger had dark hair and always wore a suit coat and tie. He was neither ugly nor handsome. I couldn't imagine him cheering on the Buffalo Bills football team, nor could I imagine him bare chested and dancing at a disco. He was a perfect blank slate of what I imagined a counselor was supposed to be. He listened carefully from behind his glasses, jotted notes in a spiral notebook, and prompted me to tell him about my crushes. I told him that although I had a girlfriend, I was also attracted to men.

"All sexual arousal is part of a pattern," he said in a dry, clinical monotone. "When anyone has fantasies that lead to arousal, then a pattern is established."

From his high-backed black leather chair, his dark eyes locked with mine, lacking judgment, pity, or compassion. "Deviant sexual arousal patterns—say when an individual is aroused by children, or animals, or someone of the same sex—can sometimes develop in place of appropriate arousal patterns."

I was a good boy who was used to following the expectations of adults and authority figures. I listened to Dr. Roger, nodded, and went home pondering this new information. It felt good to finally be honest with an adult. I had always placed trust in the adults around me, and I trusted Dr. Roger. Although attending the sessions had started at least in part as a way of getting Mom and Dad to leave me alone and not ask me uncomfortable questions about how I was feeling, I looked forward to my weekly sessions with Dr. Roger, who I could tell was just trying to help.

As a licensed psychiatrist, Dr. Roger would have followed the professional practices and standards of the American Psychiatric Association. Until 1973, homosexuality was considered a mental disorder by the APA, a position that had gone unchallenged for decades. But in 1973, a task force within the APA proposed that the Diagnostic and Statistical Manual of Mental Disorders, or DSM, no longer use that particularly odious classification. The APA's board of trustees agreed with the decision to remove the classification of homosexuality as a mental disorder, and in a vote late in 1973, fifty-eight percent of the membership agreed.

However, there were detractors. Many psychoanalysts opposed the revision. Instead of completely normalizing homosexuality, two revisions of the DSM continued to pathologize homosexuality by indicating that those who were comfortable with their homosexuality were no longer considered mentally ill; only those who were "in conflict with" their sexual orientation had a mental disorder. It wasn't until 1987, over a year after I'd become Dr. Roger's patient, that the DSM no longer labeled homosexuality a mental illness. That action was considered a watershed moment in the gay community. With that decision, gay men and women were no longer seen as ill, but up until that happened, doctors had told their gay patients that they were sick. And their professional practice standards supported them.

I will never know for sure where Dr. Roger stood in relation to all this controversy within his profession. He knew from our sessions that I was expressing anxiety about my sexual orientation, so I fit into that group of patients who were "in conflict with" their sexual orientation. Dr. Roger had a plan for making me better. There was a simplicity to his solution for my particular brand of deviance: look at photographs of women and masturbate. By doing this, he assured me, I could change my sexual arousal pattern, and that would be that. It was textbook behavior modification, a term I wouldn't learn until I took a psychology course the next year in college.

"Everything will work out fine," he said, ushering me out the door.

But I wasn't supposed to masturbate either. As the Christian Brothers liked to remind us, the catechism was clear even on that topic, which was defined as "an intrinsically and gravely disordered action…. The deliberate use of the sexual faculty, for whatever reason, outside of marriage is essentially contrary to its purpose." So how was I going to follow through on Dr. Roger's orders to masturbate to photos of scantily clad women?

I convinced myself that if I masturbated thinking of Calvin Klein underwear models, it was somehow a double sin and that I was very clearly going to hell. If I went to school and an upperclassman called me a faggot under his breath, or I got pushed in the senior hall between classes, or teased in the locker room, I was convinced that each of those actions was a direct punishment from God for having a tall, dark, and handsome underwear model in my thoughts the night before.

I made a decision that I would have to risk whatever displeasure God had in store for me and engage in some limited sinful behavior in the short run. I could always go to confession for forgiveness in order to save my everlasting soul.

I remembered that my friend from around the corner had discovered a stash of his dad's girly magazines in a bedside table. The drawer in my father's bedside table contained monogrammed handkerchiefs and collar stays for his work shirts. The shelf underneath had a Bible and some books with math puzzles in them. Mark's subscription of *Sports Illustrated* was still coming to the house, so, willing to give Elle Macpherson, Kathy Ireland, and the rest of the supermodels who showed up in the annual spread a try, I decided to search for that year's swimsuit issue.

I tried. I tried and tried. Apparently, I wasn't working nearly hard enough. The deviant arousal pattern continued. I was doomed to hell.

Chapter 7
Linda: A Family Home

"I want what you and Dad have."

There he was, on the cusp of adulthood, newly emancipated from his older brother who had gone off to college. We were in the wallpapered kitchen, which was redone in a mélange of orange and brown straight out of the late seventies. I was chopping up walnuts for my famous Italian Christmas cookies, the same ones I made every year that my family dutifully ate without complaint. Christopher was in his senior year at St. Joe's in 1985. I thought he'd enjoy this year without his brother around. Mark is funny and gregarious, often the center of attention. Sadly, that year Christopher, often alone in his bedroom, seemed reclusive. Depressed, maybe. I didn't know why.

His statement about wanting what his dad and I had puzzled me. Of course you can have this I thought. We just have an ordinary married life. Why on earth can't you have that? What I learned much later, to my great sadness, was that he was struggling with his sexuality. For a teenager in our devout family, who was attending a conservative Catholic school in very conservative blue collar Buffalo in the 1980s, that was no easy feat.

Back when we moved to North Buffalo in 1973, I was thrilled

that we could have such a nice middle-class house in such a nice neighborhood. It was what I always wanted. The kind of house that might have belonged to Dick and Jane from my first and second grade readers. In my childhood home we had no white picket fence, no dad with a briefcase nor a mother who wore a dress with pearls to prepare dinner. Dad carried a tin lunch bucket to the factory, and Mom wore faded cotton house dresses. I guess I wanted the type of life featured in those fifties sitcoms *Ozzie and Harriet* and *Leave it to Beaver*. No, I did not wear pearls. Nor did we have that white picket fence. We did have a two-story, middle class house of the kind I had longed for in my youth.

Like most of our gang of friends, Bob and I had married early, when we were almost 23 years old in 1965. Our college friends all married that same summer, a year after we graduated from college. We were in each other's weddings and our group of five couples started having children right away. Because I was pregnant with my first son after only two and a half years of teaching, I had to resign. In those long-ago days, women teachers were required to take a leave or resign when they were four months pregnant. I believed, of course, that I would be a stay-at-home mom like my mom and all the other women in my family. So, after Mark was born in 1967, I quit teaching. I was so sure about this that I withdrew the sum of money I had already accumulated in the teachers' retirement program. In my family, and in my own mind, mothers had to be available for their kids.

Betty Friedan's 1963 book *The Feminine Mystique* began to trickle into backwater Buffalo. My women friends began to read it and pass it around. In that same year, President Kennedy signed the Equal Pay Act into law. In 1966, the National Organization for Women (NOW) was formed. In the early seventies, NOW and other women's groups lobbied for opportunity in lending for women, for an end to pregnancy discrimination and, most famously, for legal abortion. So, the winds of change affected me as our family moved to our home on Parkside Avenue in 1973. Soon I would take the momentous step of working full-time which would change us all.

Even though I may have wished for a new path, I also wanted a fun, nurturing household for my boys. I did not want my children to experience the operatic stress that seemed common in my childhood. My own mother enforced rules on my sister and me with the wooden spoon on the behind. Spankings were the way to control children then, so my mom was not unusual. My growing up world was very narrow and restricted. We rarely traveled, never went to plays or on vacations. And there always seemed to be lots of upheaval. Arguments, tears, anger. Money worries.

Not what I wanted for my precious sons! I did not want grandparents living with us sucking up all our energy. I did not want the fainting, the smelling salts, the breakdowns that my mother was prone to. I did not want the arguments between my alcoholic grandfather and my long-suffering mother. Though I never doubted that I was loved and valued growing up, I may have been insensitive to the fact that illness and lack of money could exacerbate many family problems. Now I just wanted more for my own kids. That is what all parents want for their families.

Of course we had our own nuclear-family arguments, tears,

and anger. Can't be the Beaver's family all the time or even most of the time. But I loved our home. Each son had his own bedroom. No sharing as I had done.

We lived only half a block from St. Rose of Lima Church. As we did in my family, Bob and I centered our growing family around the church. We went to Mass every Sunday and celebrated all the sacraments. Our sons even attended Catholic schools for most of their education. We really believed religious schools were vital to their spiritual lives. Both Bob and I were very devout Catholics and even served in leadership positions in our church. I served on the liturgy committee and taught religious education. Bob helped facilitate volunteer opportunities to soup kitchens.

Of course each child in a family is unique. Christopher seemed like a happy, active kid most of the time, though he was perhaps more reserved than his brother. Mark is only a year older, so I often dressed them alike and treated them like twins. I did not take a good look at their differences. When Christopher was almost four, he developed a strange illness. For about a week he grew increasingly listless and slept for long periods of time. We took him to the pediatrician, who could find nothing wrong. After another week, my lively child, who talked early and walked early, was beginning to lose both abilities. He drooled, could barely walk, and could not speak clearly. Both Bob and I were beyond frantic. Again it felt as if someone I loved had fallen off the map.

Again I brought Christopher to the pediatrician. The doctor closed the blinds, turned off the lights, peered deeply into his eyes, and said, "Take him to the hospital right away." While at Children's Hospital, Christopher had a spinal tap that confirmed a diagnosis of encephalitis. By that time, he was in a wheelchair and barely speaking. Since it was a virus, there were no medicines to treat it. Bob and I took turns staying overnight with him. Miracle of miracles, he recovered. But I'm not sure I ever did! That existential fear every parent dreads stayed with me for a long time. The day we brought him home from the hospital, one of Bob's students visited and told us of her family member who never recovered and was permanently confined to a nursing home. My hands shook.

To me, both our boys were (and are) bright, funny, and resourceful, capable of devising lots of different projects. One of Mark's was to collect hats. He wrote about it for *Highlights*, a magazine for children, and got his first press clipping at about seven or eight years old. Christopher was always planning plays for holiday gatherings. He would rope in Mark and their cousins for rehearsals during most of Christmas Day. Then all the adults were called to the basement to see the play. I loved it. They were being creative. And they stayed out of my way while I tried to cook dinner for a houseful of relatives.

Both boys participated in Little League baseball. I wanted to encourage them in sports, especially since I am not athletic. In fact, I am not good at any sport. I tried tennis as an adult and was a miserable failure. I did not even learn to swim. While Christopher did not seem too enthusiastic about Little League, he did participate. I thought if he learned to play baseball, he could learn to play tennis or golf, and maybe that would be good for him as an adult. I did not want him, as I am, to be on the sidelines for anything athletic. It's interesting that we project some of our insufficiencies onto our children, not considering what they want.

High school was a different story. By then, Mark was pushing his way into adolescence, and dodging his parents was one way to do that. Issues like broken curfews and drinking bouts erupted. Christopher, on the other hand, was more withdrawn and remote. This was its own cause for concern.

Until Christopher was in high school, I did not think he was sad. He did seem more sensitive than his brother. So I think I spent more time with him than with Mark. Also, Christopher's severe illnesses as a child made me possibly more attentive to him. But he did not dwell on any illness. Until high school, he was the one in the family who was most eager to join creative projects. He might come up with them or I might. He was the one who lobbied for Christmas decorations early. One year, on his demand, we had these cheesy, blinking neon Christmas lights in the window. Both boys helped make all the ornaments for the Christmas tree. He liked to bake, too, which was great since I loved a partner in that endeavor. He also played the piano and joined the Boy Scouts.

Our neighborhood was tight-knit. In addition, my parents and my sister and her family were only a mile away. This was much as I remember my childhood in our multigenerational two-family home. Though I did not want my parents living with me, as my mother's parents had with her, I was glad that they were close by. I thought that kids needed many adults around who loved them. My parents fussed over my sons, playing games, preparing special meals for them, encouraging them to stay overnight at their home.

They thoroughly enjoyed having them around and were eager to take them on adventures, picking strawberries, having ice cream, or going on picnics.

Both sets of grandparents were valued additions to our sons' lives and gave Bob and me time to spend with our friends. We often had Sunday dinners at their homes. We shared household tasks like painting or home repair. We often stopped in to visit each other. We even had keys to each other's home and could pop in unannounced. The values of a close loving family were important to me, and I wanted that for my children. We were often with Bob's family, too, but they lived farther away, so we had to make special plans to visit them. We often traveled with Bob's brother and his family. Family life was and is very important to us.

Sometimes I chafed at the closeness, though. I couldn't leave the dishes around or take a nap in the afternoon without wondering if my family would stop in. They would visit the kids several times during the week. That was fine before I went back to work. As a working mom, I had lots to do at night. Sitting around talking to my parents wasn't high on my agenda. They were so loving and so eager to help that I felt I could not say anything to them. Maybe it would have been better for all of us if I had been more honest with them. But I did not want to impair in any way their relationship with my boys.

Though our immediate neighbors were staunch, traditional Catholics, Bob and I were greatly influenced by the liberalization in the Church wrought by Vatican II, which lasted far beyond its brief years of 1961 to 1964. I read the newest Catholic theology by liberal theologians such as Hans Kung and Karl Rahner. When we gathered with our neighbors, we often had debates about our different views of the Catholic Church. Our neighbors rued the loss of the Latin Mass, which confounded Bob and me. We loved the changes and started attending what was called the folk Mass at a local college. There we heard stimulating sermons based on social justice along with zippy new songs, not the traditional old hymns. So, though our neighborhood was Catholic, there were competing views. Despite this, I loved the neighborhood and loved the house. It was filled with our kids, their friends and our family. I remember looking out the back window one day and seeing my boys running bases with the neighbor kids. I smiled to myself. This was what I wanted.

In our professional lives, we were committed to teaching in the public schools, which were just beginning to address the long-term gerrymandering that made some schools all white and others almost all black. Bob was recruited to work on a plan to implement the desegregation order that had come down from Federal Court. As a math teacher, his skills were needed to look at the statistics in the Buffalo Public Schools and to work on devising ways to integrate the schools.

Before Christopher was in high school, he attended Campus East, which was a new magnet middle school. We sensed that he was in his brother's shadow at St. Rose Elementary School. Unfortunately, they were only a year apart. So at each grade, Christopher got compared to his more outgoing brother.

Bob and I were involved with the new magnet schools in

Buffalo, and we thought attending Campus East would be a nice change for Christopher. Now that I realize he was bullied, though he never complained, which makes me even sadder. Perhaps he encountered more because other kids may have sensed he was different. With social media this kind of bullying is even more common today.

On the plus side at Campus East, Christopher took music lessons, joined the swim team, and, maybe best of all for him, was in the class plays. His teachers at Campus East were thrilled with him. He received lots of accolades. He won the highest achievement award upon his graduation from eighth grade. Perhaps it would not have been so challenging for him as a gay kid had we encouraged him to attend a public high school. We made a half-hearted offer to attend one of the new magnet high schools. But Mark was already in the Catholic boys' school only about a mile from our house, so Christopher decided to go there. I suppose it was mostly because we wanted him to.

It's hard to go back to our feelings and beliefs at the time. Both Bob and I, as Catholics, believed we needed to share our faith with our sons and by sending them to religious schools, we were doing that. In fact, when I was in high school, the nuns inculcated in us this need for religious education. We were often warned that attending a public college would endanger our very souls. They even refused to send transcripts to the University of Buffalo at that time. I guess that's why I went to D'Youville.

Of course Bob and I valued public education. How could we not? We taught in public schools and believed in them. However, our Catholic faith came first. Our group of friends felt the same way. All of them sent their children to Catholic schools. Now it probably seems a quaint belief. It was powerful back then. This is clear from just the number of religious schools in existence in both Buffalo and the surrounding areas at that time. It has all changed now. Many Catholic schools have closed. The remaining ones are very costly. The almost free labor of teaching nuns has disappeared.

Soon after he entered high school, Christopher seemed to form a great community of friends among students in both the musical plays and the chorus. I helped with makeup on the musicals and the camaraderie there seemed terrific. I suppose it seems ridiculous now, but I did not know the drama club was the gathering place for gay teens. Since some of the football players were also in the plays, I was impressed that the arts were attractive to all students. Again, gay issues were just not in my world-view at that time. Later, when I began to take more advanced courses in women's studies at the University of Buffalo, that would change. And, of course, Christopher pushed that change.

When they were at St. Joe's High School, I thought that my sons had found their different paths, Mark in rowing and Christopher in the plays. But I did sense that Christopher was quiet and often aloof. Especially in his junior and senior years. I worried about his being eclipsed by his more extroverted brother in our extended family. I knew that my parents and my sister loved both my boys. But Mark seemed to command more of their attention. He was funny and outgoing and loved to tease them.

I worried a lot. But I didn't know what to do. I think I went out of my way to bring Christopher's achievements to the family's attention. It was lame. And I am sure it seemed forced.

Though I saw myself as a very liberal educated woman, gay issues just weren't impinging on my consciousness then. Consequently, when Christopher was in high school, I did not really understand what was going on. He was and is such a lovable guy. He went to the family dinners. He participated in school plays. He went to Mass with us on Sundays. But it was clear that something was wrong. He spent lots of time alone in his room. As a high school teacher, I had seen depressed kids. And I knew of kids dying by suicide. Plus there seemed to be the stain of depression in my family. My mother had severe anxiety, I was prone to depression, and other family members were heavy drinkers, which oftentimes masks depression, or so I've read. Also, Christopher had asthma and allergies when he was young. In fact he had been hospitalized for severe breathing problems. Our allergist at the time really helped him. She was so focused on the damage caused by undiagnosed allergies that she had me convinced they could cause all kinds of personality changes, too. She had written books on the subject, which I consulted religiously. I feared his health may have caused this depression.

It's painful to read now about how Christopher struggled. I so wish I had handled it all differently. Did I know he was gay? It's a question that has been asked of me and that I have asked myself. What about that incident wearing my shoes when he was young? Should that have made me wonder? I vaguely remembered it until he wrote about it. What did I think then? Not sure. Maybe I thought it was just a child playing dress up. Or maybe I suppressed the memory, because at that time I did not want to consider that my young son might be somehow different

So I went on as usual but prayed a lot. Following the model of the women in my family who used prayer to deal with difficult issues. To jolly Christopher out of his blues, I tried to be funny at times. Finally, we decided as a family to consult a therapist. But that was after he made that statement that I did not understand until years later.

"I want what you and Dad have."

Chapter 8
A Note from Dad

March 16, 2014

Son,

I just read your latest installment of your blog, and I never want to be an editor for any content that you or mom write. Whatever you feel or felt growing up is there, and I know that you would never intentionally hurt either of us. I think that what the two of you are doing is fantastic, and I only hope that it does get to be the basis for a book.

Please remember that today is a much different time than the 1960s or 70s. What did I know about "gender" roles having one brother and no sisters? What did Mom know about boys having just one sister?

We certainly didn't think much about gender as we tried to raise happy kids while both working to be able to give you and Mark some things we didn't have growing up.

Son, as you struggled in high school and college, I struggled with my inability to say to you, "Is there anything you want to talk with me about?" If I didn't know for sure that you were gay or at least wondering, I certainly had my suspicions. To this day I am sorry that I was not more open to you back then. If anything, I was afraid for what that might mean for you. The AIDS epidemic was a concern, and certainly society's view of gays was a problem. I apologize for never being the one to openly discuss this with you.

I love you dearly, and there was never a time that I didn't.

Chapter 9
Christopher: Closet

*All we have to do now
Is take these lies and make them true somehow....
Well it looks like the road to heaven
But it feels like the road to hell*
—George Michael, "Freedom"

To get started in college, I had to drive 180 miles west on I-90 to John Carroll, a Catholic Jesuit university in University Heights, a suburb of Cleveland, Ohio. Everything about John Carroll was so familiar: the upper-middle-class white students who attended, the emphasis on both studying and socializing, the Mass on Sunday. John Carroll ended up being a popular school of choice in Buffalo. Several students with whom I'd graduated from St. Joe's were also going there, as were some female friends and acquaintances from St. Joe's sister schools.

By the middle of freshman year, I had found my way to the campus newspaper office where I worked as a reporter. It was at the newspaper that I found my first friends. Bridget, the editorial page editor, was an upperclassman who was smart, cynical, and funny. Keith was the editor in chief. He smoked cigarettes and, critical of anything and everything they did, was a general thorn in the side of the school administration. Our sports reporter, Chris, was a freshman like me. Gregarious and outgoing, he knew every athlete on campus. Although at first I thought we had absolutely nothing in common, he ended up becoming one of my best college friends.

It was Karen, who looked exactly like young, beautiful Jessica Lange in the movie *Tootsie*, who became my obsession. She was wicked smart and driven, a year older than me and also an English major. Together, we studied the great texts of British literature and burned the midnight oil writing articles for the *Carroll News*. By my sophomore year we were a couple. She and I visited my family in Buffalo during spring break, and on a road trip that summer to Milwaukee to meet her family, we sang show tunes out the window and talked of the future.

The newspaper staff became my family. We ate meals together in the cafeteria, studied together in the library, drank together at local bars while debating Ronald Reagan's trickle-down economic policy, and talking about how appalled we were about the Iran-Contra Affair. My friends at the newspaper and I would take a break from working on our deadlines to go to the last-chance Mass on Sunday nights at ten o'clock, which was a social event in and of itself. It was them I went to, distraught, when I discovered during my sophomore year that my roommates had dressed up in my clothes and taken pictures of themselves reading my journal.

In pictures from that time, I am smiling, laughing, and often clearly inebriated, enjoying the freedom of college, that rite of passage into adulthood for many in America. I was still trying as hard as I could, however, to be straighter than before, still carrying Dr.

Roger's advice with me, still intent on denying my attraction to men, still working to alter my sexual arousal pattern. I was never forthcoming with my friends at the *Carroll News* and didn't even write about these feelings in my private journal, the one saving grace when it was read by those assholes.

Despite my efforts, the attraction I felt toward men wasn't lessening. I sought counseling from an older Jesuit priest on campus. It was winter of my sophomore year, and I crept quietly to his office in a faculty residence hall, a place students never entered. I didn't want anyone to see me. What would I say if a friend or classmate happened by and asked why I was ringing the bell at the Jesuit residence? That I was just popping in to discuss Chaucer with Fr. James over tea? But that was the purpose of office hours, of course, and those happened in the office building, not the Jesuit residence. The dark wood of the residence hall gleamed of linseed oil and history, a reminder of the Carmelite monastery of my youth. While a cold, Cleveland winter sun shone through leaded glass windows, I slowly told my story, tentatively mentioning depression, a lack of interest, a struggle with finding my place.

My confessor, I can't remember his name, was old and balding. He asked me a few questions that seemed rote and basic. Finally, I mentioned that perhaps I wasn't always attracted to women. Perhaps I was different. What if I was? I struggled to put into words the feelings I was having, to clearly state the condition of my mind and my soul, and he struggled to keep his eyes open. His head bobbed. Or was it a nod of understanding? Then his eyes stayed closed for a few seconds too long. I guess he had heard it all before. It didn't occur to me to be angry. I took it as a sign that my problems were nothing compared with the suffering of Our Lord and Savior Jesus Christ.

On my return from a semester abroad in London during my junior year, I found out that Karen was dating someone else. I engaged in a feeble attempt to get her back but was secretly relieved. I kept up the façade and dated a few other women. I made new friends outside the newspaper circle, drank too much, and smoked pot for the first time. I never told anyone that I was anything other than what I presented myself as: a straight young man interested in women.

During my senior year, I moved into a rental house off campus with Geoff, a friend from high school, and Chris, from the newspaper staff. Chris made everyone around him laugh. We danced at the charity dance-a-thon and traveled to college newspaper conferences in New York. We talked politics and school gossip and New Wave music. The only thing I was never interested in was sitting down at night or on the weekend to watch a football game. I was drawn to Chris because he is smart, thoughtful, and kind, nonjudgmental and a good listener. Even so, I never once mentioned to him in all our years at John Carroll that I might be gay.

I continued to hold back from sharing that with anyone close to me. I built a wall around my inner self during college that kept my secret inside and left others out. It wasn't until after graduation, as society began to change and many of us moved away from our Catholic roots, that the dam broke and half a dozen of us in my graduating class tentatively came out of the closet. I don't know the specifics of what kept them closeted. Was it the fact that we were all at this conservative Catholic university? That we all worried about acceptance from families and friends? That the barely concealed homophobia in the 1980s left all of us fearful for our physical safety? It was probably a combination of all of these.

Meanwhile, as graduation approached in 1990, I took some tentative steps down the road of rebellion. I grew my hair long. I watched classmates get dressed in suits for interviews with insurance companies and accounting firms, while I wore black turtlenecks and a brown leather jacket. And, having answered an ad on the back page of a local alternative weekly magazine, I had my first real date with a man.

I knew nothing of the real world. Every young woman I had ever dated was connected in some way to the web of social contacts that I had spun for myself or, more accurately, that had been spun for me by the schools I attended and the neighborhood where we lived. I had been cloistered by my Catholic world.

That changed on a Saturday evening some months before graduation. I climbed into my car and drove across the city to the apartment of a man I did not know. Before the age of the internet, gay men had only a few choices for meeting and hooking up with one another. There were bars and clubs, but I wasn't in the habit of going out alone, and I didn't know anyone who was out and gay at school even if I had wanted to reach out. I'm sure there was cruising that happened at some parks or other public places, but I was a bit too buttoned up for that. Who am I kidding? I probably didn't even know what cruising was at the time.

What I did know was that men looking to meet other men for companionship (and sex) sometimes met one another through classified ads in the local newspaper. This gentleman I was planning to meet had placed his ad on the back pages of the alternative weekly in a column I had been reading religiously for months. I wrote a short reply, sealed it into an envelope, and sent it off. Before texts and social media and dating apps, the United States Postal Service was the way in which my first date with a gay man was arranged. I seem to recall that there were also messages being left on a voicemail service the paper provided. He sounded nice enough.

As I drove away from my house in University Heights, I passed through streets that were familiar to me from my years at John Carroll University, streets that were lined with middle-class homes similar to the one I had grown up in back in Buffalo. Slowly I made my way downtown, an area I knew only from quick glimpses as my friends and I sped past on our way to and from bars in the Flats along the Cuyahoga River.

Pulling the car over several times to check the map, I had to navigate through streets I had never been down before and finally parked in front of a three-story apartment building surrounded by a jumble of others that looked exactly like it. The man who answered the doorbell was tall, broad-shouldered, and held the door open for me with a warm smile. He was African American and about ten years older than I, neither of which he had shared previously. It's okay, I thought, trying not to display the fact that I was caught unawares. It's not a big deal. I'm sure he's a nice guy. I'm cool with this.

We chatted at the kitchen table of his small apartment, and he offered me a glass of wine, which probably impressed me since I was used to drinking three-dollar twelve-packs of Busch Lite. I downed it.

"What are your thoughts?" he asked coyly.

What are my thoughts? When can we kiss? What do your arms feel like wrapped around my chest? Is this going to happen?

"I was thinking about this paper that I have to write for poetry class on Monday."

I don't think this was the kind of flirting he imagined.

Luckily, he kissed me anyway. At some point, we moved to his bedroom. There, he wanted to do things that were surely deviant, and although my body was communicating a deep desire to continue, shame and guilt found their way through the narrow pathways of my mind, edging themselves nearer, more present, crowding out the rush and thrill and excitement of being there, lying beside a man, kissing him and touching him and having him kiss and touch me. And slowly there was doubt. I wasn't sure I wanted it to continue. Was this the kind of life I pictured for myself? Dates arranged with strange men I had met through an ad in the newspaper? How would I explain my absence tonight to Chris and Geoff and the rest of my friends? What would the priest say when I went to confess this sin?

Doubt and in large part fear filled my mind. Who was this guy? What if he wanted to hurt me? And then another fear, one faced by many gay and bisexual men at the time: what if I get AIDS tonight and end up losing my life?

From 1981, when the first case of AIDS was documented, until the end of 2000, the Centers for Disease Control reported that almost three quarters of a million people in the United States had been diagnosed with the disease. More than half a million had died because of it. Men who had sex with other men were the biggest group of individuals infected by the disease during that time period.

I didn't know the HIV status of the man whose apartment I visited that night. It wasn't one of the things we discussed over his kitchen table. When we went to his room, he had not mentioned his intent to use a condom. Leaving that particular encounter may very well have saved my life. Or perhaps not. I will never know.

Jumping up from the bed, I said, "I have to go."

Despite his entreaties, I made excuses, put my shirt back on, and fled. I drove back home, and once on streets I recognized, I parked the car, rolled down the window, and tried to breathe.

On the night before graduation some weeks later, I got completely drunk and, the next day, had to wear a pair of sunglasses to weave my way across the stage and receive my diploma. Mom and Dad, all four of my grandparents, and my aunt and uncle and cousin cheered from the crowd. Mark was not there; he had left for the Peace Corps earlier that year. Afterward, over dinner at Mama Santa's, our favorite place in Cleveland's Little Italy, my newspaper friends and our families toasted with carafes of red wine. I never told anyone—friends, roommates, my family—about my date.

The next day, I packed up my belongings, got into my parents' car and travelled east on I-90 to Buffalo and my old bedroom.

There, on a bed I had occupied since I was four years old, I curled up, slept, and felt, at least temporarily, safe. I didn't need to commence the next phase of my life until tomorrow.

Chapter 10
Christopher: Spring

Describing the once indescribable can dismantle the power of taboo. To speak about the once unspeakable can make the invisible familiar if repeated often enough in clear and loud tones.
—David Wojnarowicz, *Close To The Knives: A Memoir of Disintegration*

After college, I moved back to Buffalo. I lived for almost a year in an apartment on Hertel Avenue, not far from Mom and Dad. There was an imported-food store below the apartment, owned by an older Italian guy who had let the apartment go to hell but didn't charge much rent. I drove a secondhand silver Toyota Supra that had a sunroof but a malfunctioning gas gauge. "It gets exactly one hundred miles on a full tank," the guy who sold it to me said. I carried a spare gas can with me and, because I wasn't as careful as I needed to be about keeping track of the miles, used it frequently.

My uncle hired me to work part time in his rare coin shop, even though I knew absolutely nothing about rare coins. While he was out buying up estates and making sales, I sat at the front counter and prayed that nobody would wander in. Sometimes, I was tasked with polishing wheat pennies, rare one-cent coins that had Abe Lincoln's profile on one side and two stalks of wheat on the other. Other times I had to tuck trading cards between protective sleeves. Everything seemed old and worn and useless.

One day, while rummaging in the back room, I found a stack of years-old *Penthouse* magazines. The wonderful thing about *Penthouse*, at least for me, was that instead of just page after page of naked women, it had at least one feature that pictured a man and a woman, or perhaps a man and several women. Still, there he would be: a British redcoat, ready to have his way with a household of Virginia colonists; a hippie ready to deflower some nubile young flower child. There, for all to see, were actual naked men. Sure, they were engaged in sex with women, but still. Real, live men. Muscled. Hard. Beautiful.

After almost a year living on Hertel, I moved into an apartment off Elmwood Avenue. One night, thrilled with anticipation and dread, I circled Cathode Ray, a gay bar, from the safety of my car. I parked. I approached the bar, turned around, and walked back to my car. I drove away but soon realized it was now or never. I turned a corner and headed back to the bar. Inside, I met Neil. We danced. We kissed. We went back to his place and kissed some more.

That spring, I spent a lot of time at Neil's kissing, listening to Stan Getz records, and watching as Neil created collages of old photos and other strange memorabilia. Neil was an artist, and I wanted to be an actor, and, my God, there were gay artists and straight writers and all manner of actors and filmmakers in Buffalo. These people went to parties at Neil's apartment on the second floor of a wonderful old two-family home in Allentown, where they talked and laughed and eyed one another.

Outside of Neil's apartment, the world opened up after the winter, the trees budded barely pink, and the sunshine was finally warm. Mom had shared with me one of her favorite poets, Mary Oliver, whose work I had never read in college because, as it seemed, we focused on the works of only dead white males. Oliver wrote in her poem "Wild Geese" that "You only have to let the soft animal of your body / love what it loves." It felt like that was what I was doing that spring. The world offered itself to my imagination, calling to me like Oliver's wild geese, announcing my place in the family of things.

I don't know if I ever truly loved Neil. I loved the feeling of being with him. I loved how the birds sang that spring, really sang, just like they do in the movies when love happens for the first time, when the main character is truly and completely happy for the first time in a long, long time.

I invited Neil to Mom and Dad's house for dinner one night, but he was just Neil, a friend I had met through my new theater friends. Mom cooked. We drank beers and discussed politics and films and art. It was much like all the other dinners with family and friends that I had shared around that dining room table for as long as I could remember except that, when it was over, Neil and I went back to his apartment, where we kissed and probably laughed about how we had successfully evaded suspicion. Or had we? I always wondered if Mom and Dad had any idea.

So that I could interview for jobs, because even artists needed to pay rent, Mom and I went to Men's Wearhouse, where she purchased a gray pinstripe suit for me. But the suit went mostly unused. Instead of getting a job where a suit was required, I started substitute teaching in Buffalo Public Schools during the day and working behind a deli counter on nights and weekends. I was twenty-three years old, and much closer in age to the high school students I was teaching than to the teachers with whom I shared the lunchroom.

I frequently took substitute-teaching jobs at Hutch Tech, where Mom was teaching English. The school was less than a mile from my apartment, so I could roll out of bed in the morning and make it to school with a cup of coffee in hand in less than thirty minutes. After school sometimes, Mom and I would stop for tea at the Towne Restaurant, one of the many Greek diners in Buffalo, where we would split a baklava and talk about politics or movies or my tentative steps to become a part of the small but flourishing acting scene in town.

We also talked about Mom's increased responsibilities in caring for her parents, who were getting older and starting to slow down. One day, because my grandfather had set up some ladders and started to clean the gutters on their house, my grandmother called Mom in a panic. Once he was up there, as it turned out, he'd started feeling dizzy. Then his asthma had kicked in. Dad had to rush over to lend a hand with the gutters, and Mom had to calm her mother. It was in Mom's retelling of this event that I learned more about my grandmother's mental breakdowns years before and understood something about the resentment and frustration that Mom and my Aunt Judy felt about having to care for their mother when they were young.

"Your grandmother has been a wonderful grandmother to you and your brother and your cousin," Mom told me, "but she wasn't always easy to live with when your aunt and I were growing up."

It was also during these conversations that I began to learn about some of Mom's aunts and great-aunts who had suffered physical abuse at the hands of domineering and alcoholic husbands. My grandmother's fragile mental state started to make more sense when I learned that, as the only daughter in a traditional Italian American family, she was expected to care for her ailing mother and deal with an alcoholic, philandering father.

The stories of the women in Mom's family, part of her blood and mine, found their way into Mom's poetry, something she had started to work on after Mark and I left for college. Confining Dad's papers and our family records to a filing cabinet in the corner, she took over the tiny spare room at the end of the hall and claimed it as her own. She set up a desk and tacked postcards of the Impressionist painter Mary Cassatt's work on a board above it. She photocopied poems by Mary Oliver and Audre Lorde, her idols, and plastered them on the board next to the postcards.

Mom showed off her office to me one day when I was over doing laundry and eating dinner. She was both proud and defiant. "When I'm in here with the door closed, your dad knows that he better not bother me."

Mom also had one of her own poems on the board by the desk. Titled "Leda's Song," it revealed the plight of a great-aunt:

*At thirteen when I began to bleed
Momma found me a husband
because there was little food
in the house on Jefferson Street.
She said he would care for me,
it was time to make room
for the younger ones,
save precious bread and wine.*

*I bore him three sons
in quick bursts,
yet my peppers and eggs
were never quite right.
The bread did not rise
into light flaky loaves
like momma's.
Besides Joe would drink wine
to fuel his anger at his poverty
until hitting me became his joy
--his way of loving himself.*

*During one of Momma's tea sessions
Papa saw my bruises
His grey handlebar moustache quivered
Let it be Papa, I have three kids,
besides Momma says I must cook better.
Papa went after him with a shotgun
but by then it was too late.
My last beating broke all my ribs.
One punctured my lungs
and the end rushed in
to save me.*

I was shocked when I read Leda's story. She couldn't be real.

She seemed to be a character straight out of a novel or the movies. Other poems laid bare the lives of my great-grandmother and other great-aunts and distant cousins. Coming to know them and their stories through Mom's poems filled me with sorrow and anger. We had women in our family who suffered these indignities?

Family as I knew it was loving, supportive, welcoming. Men of an older generation, men like both of my grandfathers, doted on their wives, catered to their every need, worked hard to provide a better life than what they had grown up with, and their American dream had for all intents and purposes come true. They had done better. They lived in comfort, with much more than they had started off, and their marriages seemed strong, loving, and lasting. My aunts and grandmothers and mother didn't seem to be the kind of women who would put up with shit from anyone, and certainly not their husbands. None of them struck me as the kind of women who suffered in silence. But what did I know? Were there more secrets locked away, whispered out of the earshot of young men?

"There's an old Italian saying," Mom told me when we discussed how much I loved her poems. She was hesitant about writing, afraid to share her work too widely. She even ended up carefully curating the poems she showed her mother, afraid Ma would disapprove.

"You don't air your dirty laundry in public," she said. "You don't risk your precious status in society. For the sake of your family, you put a carefully crafted image forward to the world and save face."

For Mother's Day that year, I bought Mom dangly earrings

unlike anything I had seen her wear before. She loved them. She bought herself a full, brightly colored skirt, also unlike anything I had seen her wear before, and wore both the skirt and the earrings to her first poetry reading. One of the poems she read that night was "Confident Women."

> *The confident women are tall and*
> *Have red hair they fling about like Medusa*
> *And tight jeans grabbing their crotch*
> *So they can feel their sex*
> *Openly and without apology.*
> *They talk loudly and say:*
> *I don't care what anybody thinks.*
> *And I sit on the sidewalk*
> *Playing jacks, snatching them up*
> *In hesitant sweeps*
> *And ask mother may I, may I?*
>
> *I look up as they sway just a bit of hip*
> *In an easy breeze of summer on Elmwood Ave.*
> *They have zigzag paper in their purses*
> *Along with pills and a large rubber O.*
> *Their leather jackets hang askew*
> *As they toss ribbons of hair aside*
> *Thrust a finger at the shouting hardhats.*
>
> *I grow smaller on the pavement*
> *Shrink, shrivel from their high voices.*
> *One jumps on a passive motorcycle*
> *Strokes it into power and zooms her escape.*
> *Another flicks open the door of a sportscar*
> *To grab the shift and plunge it alive*
> *Off hot sticky clutching pavement.*
> *The last lounges on the sidewalk*

> *In a webbed chair in front of her shop*
> *She thrusts aside her shirt to nurse*
> *The newborn child, the new me.*

This poem shocked me. Who was this poet? Certainly not *my* mother. Zig-Zag paper and rubber Os and motorcycles were all things that I didn't even know Mom knew about. Until Mom explained it to me, in fact, I didn't even know what Zig-Zag paper was. I suppose part of becoming an adult is when you realize that your own parents are real, actual people just like yourself, with hopes and dreams and hidden longings. This poet was someone more akin to a friend, someone like one of my college friends with whom I might spend late nights drinking in a dark corner of a trashy Cleveland bar.

I *loved* this person, my new friend.

It was around this time that I was cast in a play being produced by the University of Buffalo Theatre Department. Also in the cast was a beautiful young woman named Caitlin. We became fast friends, and soon I decided I wanted to be more than friends. I wooed, begged even, and finally won her over. I dove into the relationship with fervor, devoting myself to her. I met and got close to her family, playing the role of boyfriend so well I even convinced Mom and Dad that it was serious. "I thought you were on the way to marrying her," Mom later confided. I almost convinced myself that men were a thing of the past.

The winter after we began dating, I was cast in the play *The Boys in the Band* as Harold, the flaming queen whose friends throw a surprise-party-cum-bitch-fest for his birthday. To the world, I was a straight man who had been entrusted to play this quintessentially gay role, and I approached it with amateurish Method devotion. I asked the men in the cast who were out to share their insights on being gay, and they took it upon themselves to help me walk and move on stage "like a true queen would." I read books and had long talks with the director. I developed a detailed biography of the character, fleshing out a background of internalized homophobia and bullying that had shades of my own life.

In another version of my life, I might have thrown myself into the role with abandon, come out of the closet, and thanked God Almighty for allowing me this experience with all those strong, beautiful men who could be friends, mentors, and perhaps lovers. Looking back now, I can't help but think that was what the director, himself an openly gay man, had hoped all along.

Let your body love what it loves, he probably thought to himself.

One thing holding me back was the kind of life I saw some of those men living. Few of them were in committed relationships, and certainly none had children. Gay men went to bars and clubs. Most drank a good deal. Some did drugs. A few that I knew were doctors and lawyers. Of the two monogamous and committed relationships between men that I knew of, one didn't last longer than five years.

Fear still seemed to drive most gay men I knew. Fear of being beaten up outside a gay bar. Fear of being outed to one's family or employer. Fear of AIDS. Gay men had a much better understanding of the disease by the 1990s, of course, but one mistake or one less-than-completely-safe sexual encounter could still prove fatal. It wasn't until the mid-1990s that mortality rates in the LGBTQ community began to decline in the United States. The widespread use of a new type of protease inhibitor drug to treat HIV became available at that point, giving those who were HIV positive a chance at a long and healthy life.

Not only were there relatively few men to look up to as role models for the kind of life that might appeal to me, but in the early 1990s, there were also no positive, fully actualized gay male (or, for that matter, female) characters in the movies or on television. Ellen DeGeneres—and her character on the sitcom *Ellen*—came out on the cover of *Time* magazine in 1997. It wasn't until 1998 on the NBC sitcom *Will and Grace* that Will and his best friend Jack became the first leading male characters who were out. Poor Will didn't get a romantic kiss until 2005. In fact, there was a decided lack of onscreen kissing between male couples on television until *Queer as Folk* started in the United States in 2000. And that was on cable.

In my life, as well as in the media at this time, there were no male couples who had the kind of lifestyle I wanted: a committed relationship with children and a close relationship with my extended family. What's more, televangelists were still screaming about the sinful choices gay men made and the plague that God had sent to punish them, while politicians were doing only the bare minimum to help stem the public health crisis that was the AIDS epidemic. The prevailing wisdom was that gay men made choices, and with more fortitude they could come around to what was natural and right. The message was pretty clear: gays lived life in the shadows, happy and content only in their own communities, not welcome at the tables of their family or the wider community.

One brutal winter day, a day so cold and full of deep, dark snow clouds that it could only happen in Buffalo, I got into my car and crossed the Peace Bridge into Canada. I needed a break. I needed the solace of the Canadian beaches, even if they were cold. I parked the car and sat on the frozen sand staring out across Lake Erie crusted over with ice. The frigid wind pierced my clothes and burrowed deep inside me. Moved by the fierce wind off the lake and the dull, bright gray of ice and snow and sky, I started to cry.

At that moment, I honestly wanted nothing more to do with life. I had begged a beautiful woman to date me, I had grown close to her and her friends and family, and I still had a nagging desire for men. But dating men didn't seem like a viable option. It might satisfy a sexual need, but it also seemed to be a dead-end street that certainly didn't lead to other things I wanted in life.

Staring out at the cold, gray ice, I thought of my choices. I could choose suicide, but I knew it was both gutless and a ticket to hell. I could choose to continue dating Caitlin, perhaps even marry her, and then seek out men on the side to fulfill my deep sexual desires. It was a path many men had pursued for years, but the deception and duplicity that came with it were anathema to everything I believed, everything the church and my parents had taught me. It depressed me beyond belief.

If I did continue to date Caitlin, however, and continued pretending that I was straight, maybe there was a chance that something else in my life, like acting or teaching, would flip a switch and suddenly I would no longer feel incomplete. Maybe, as I hoped beyond all hope, this crisis wasn't actually about my sexual orientation. Maybe, as Dr. Roger had suggested years before, my issues would resolve themselves if I just tried hard enough and found something different to fulfill my desires. I had internalized Dr. Roger's message: find an acceptable place to attach your passions and everything will work out okay.

Driving back to Buffalo across the bridge, I tucked all my sadness and uncertainty under a smooth clear veneer and continued to play the part. I could be straight, I told myself. I would choose to be straight, and I would find a straight path to happiness for the kind of future I wanted.

I continued dating Caitlin for a while. Since I had decided to redouble my efforts to be straight, there was no way I was willing to convincingly play gay on stage. I practiced my prissy Harold walk prior to the house opening each night, but my performance in *Boys in the Band* was an utter acting failure. I watched, as if from a far-removed place, as the world called to me in its variety of ways to make change. I was strong. I resisted.

Not long after closing night, Caitlin and I split. I was sure I would never be forgiven for begging her to love me and then letting her go. I continued to act and date other women, but dreamed, too, of breaking away, getting out of Buffalo, and pursuing something new. I wanted to strike out on my own, get away from that place. I ached to be, in some way at least, free.

Chapter 11
Linda: Becoming a Feminist Woman

In women's development, the absolute of care, defined initially as not hurting others, becomes complicated through a recognition of personal integrity.
 —Carol Gilligan, *In A Different Voice*

One day you finally knew
what you had to do, and began,
though the voices around you
kept shouting
their bad advice—-
 —Mary Oliver, "The Journey"

"I'll never be like you," I shouted at my mother, as I slammed the kitchen door and left the house for a walk.

My best friend Marcia and I spent hours at Your Host, a crummy diner, eating cheese Danish, drinking coffee, smoking cigarettes. We told ourselves we would not have lives like our mothers, full-time housewives and mothers. Full-time drudges, we thought. But even with cigarette smoke on my breath, faintly masked by chewing gum, I would try to get home for family dinners because I did find them comforting, an anchor in my changing world.

Taking care of her family and her parents upstairs was Mom's life. It caused her to be what she called "nervous," which she told me every time I talked back or wanted to go out with my friends. My desire to be involved with friends seemed to threaten her. She said my rebellious behavior was making her ill, which was a frightening threat because of her earlier breakdown. In retrospect, I can see how limiting her life was. All the caretaking descended on my mom. Even in those pre-feminist times I could see that her life was not what I wanted for myself.

Of course I had no idea what I did want.

By the time I was in college, Grandma had died and Grandpa, who still lived upstairs, kept up his nightly drunks and even increased them. One incident has stayed with me. My mother and I went upstairs to confront Grandpa on his worsening drinking and the falling-down-drunk debacles Mom had to clean up after. Now she had the sole responsibility of feeding and caring for him. Because of her, his flat was spic and span with holy pictures on the wall, spare furniture, and a large oak dining room table that no one used. What started out as a conversation degenerated into shouting. Grandpa was tall and distinguished looking. But he had a loud voice and rough shoemaker's hands that would wave through the air.

Mom said, "I am not going to take care of you anymore."

Then the most amazing thing happened. He stopped yelling. And he laughed. It was a cruel laugh. I had seen him roaring drunk but never really cruel.

He laughed with a sneer and said, "You have to."

To my chagrin, she did.

Though I thought I wanted to be different from my mom when I married, I unconsciously emulated her model, especially after my children were born. But when I returned to teaching full time in the late seventies, my role in my family had to change.

At first, I tried to do it all—care for children, keep house, and make meals in addition to working full time as a teacher. I became stressed, resentful, and even depressed. It resulted in the first of several visits to a therapist. In addition to a prescription for an antidepression medication, he recommended I talk to my husband about sharing some household tasks.

Though many people do not realize it, full-time teaching is not a seven-hour day. Especially for English teachers. In addition to lesson planning, I had hours of reading and grading essays. Bob and I had to renegotiate how children and household tasks would be handled. There were some discussions between the two of us and some shouting matches, too. Okay, maybe many shouting matches. Of course Bob believed he worked hard around the house, too. He was largely responsible for mowing the lawn, throwing out the garbage, taking care of the outside of the house. He was right about that, but the constant daily tasks of laundry, cooking, child care, and house cleaning fell on me.

That was the beginning of my breaking out of an old, culturally prescribed woman's role into a (somewhat) more empowered one. And it was the beginning of the two of us renegotiating our roles. In any long marriage, I think, that has to happen, to accommodate personal growth. Though we've tangled and argued at times, we've mostly been able to work through differences, for which I feel very grateful. Bob has been a stalwart partner on my journey.

My college women friends and I talked endlessly about balancing work and family, trying to work out the many contradictions of our new working roles. Slowly but surely, all of us who married that summer of '65 returned to the work force full time. We came from families where women expected to fulfill the homemaker role. So we debated. Whether we dusted the baseboards or changed the sheets often had an almost religious imperative. Venial sin or mortal? Our discussions had a nervous energy. How often do you clean the fridge? Do you iron shirts? It felt like we were forging a new path, without a map.

Although I felt a deep-seated need to move out of my mother's and even my sister's model of women who were focused on hearth and home, I think I paid for it with recurring bouts of depression. Or maybe it was just bad genes. In any case, it didn't help that the women in my family did not quite understand what I wanted out of life, especially since we were so close. It's hard to explain to someone who has never experienced it how one feels in a depressed state. Let me just say that I have had physical pain in my life, but I think a season of depression is even worse.

The women in my family could not relate to this need to be concerned about a career. My mom and sister talked a great deal about how they had completed various household tasks, like washing windows and cleaning cupboards. As a result, I was afraid that my lack of enthusiasm for housekeeping made me a bad wife and even a bad mom as well.

Although I could not share these concerns with the women in my family, my women friends were more sympathetic. Their mothers, however, were more supportive of their careers. I am not sure why my mother was so against a woman working outside the home. Maybe because she saw her role as so fixed. But anyway it felt as if I were taking a different road.

Some years later, after Grandpa descended into dementia and his drinking worsened, the care taking became even more difficult for my mother. Grandpa refused to stay at home, went to the bars at night, then wandered about the streets of the neighborhood. More than once he was picked up by the police and brought home. One time he was found walking on a major expressway, dodging the roaring traffic. The police were getting impatient with his behavior. My dad and I kept asking Mom to see if his doctor could recommend some kind of placement for Grandpa, but she told us the doctor said there was nothing to be done. It was just old age. Even if there were, of course Grandpa would not have agreed to go into a memory care facility or any other place like that.

But that all changed one spring. Mom was leaving a relative's home after a pleasant visit. As she walked out into the warm air, she suddenly said, "Where am I?"

She panicked and could not make sense of her surroundings. She was hysterical all the way home. I was married by then. My dad called me that night so upset that I raced over to their home. She was talking quickly, but nothing made sense.

She marched up and down the living room, saying, "Where am I? Where am I?"

Dad and I were terrified. We had never seen her quite like this. I took her to her doctor's the next day. He prescribed some medications and recommended we do something about the worsening condition of my grandfather. My dad and I then went to my grandfather's doctor to see if he could recommend some care for Grandpa. To our surprise the doctor said, "I have been telling your mother for years to have him committed. He is a danger to himself and others."

The doctor was even willing to begin the proceedings to place Grandpa in a memory unit. I was stunned. *And betrayed.* How could my mother lie to us for so long? She saw it as a badge of honor. She remained loyal to her father until she had a psychotic break. I was astounded; it was as if we spoke different languages. I guess we did.

All these experiences cultivated the grounds that made me so concerned and, yes, interested in how society and family shaped women's roles. I'd known, of course, that men governed the world. I'd have to be blind not to know it. Just a glance at a newspaper with photos of the world leaders shows that. In my experience as a schoolteacher, though a largely female profession, the administrators were usually men. However, that awareness became extremely personal when my older son, Mark, went into the Peace Corps after he graduated college in 1989.

Mark left for the former Belgian Congo, stationed in an isolated village alone without even another volunteer present. Letters and packages took months. It was in 1990, before the internet. Even transatlantic calls were very rare and iffy. Communication was so drastically cut off, I worried incessantly. What if Mark got sick? What if his villagers saw him as an intrusion and harmed him? Mary Collins, in her collaborative memoir with her son Donald, *At the Broken Places*, describes Donald moving away as a geographic death. I have to say that's what it felt like to me. That existential parental fear that I had experienced many years before with Christopher's severe illness came roaring back. A falling off the map.

No one, not even my close women friends, could quite understand why I was so undone. Then the following year, Christopher said that he planned to visit Mark in the Congo and maybe join the Peace Corps himself. That made me doubly distressed.

Not too long after Christopher returned from his visit to his brother, the Congo experienced civil unrest near the region Mark was stationed. I was beside myself with worry. I called the Peace Corps office in Washington, DC. Luckily, I did get to talk to someone who was aware of the situation. I asked for an update on the safety of the volunteers in that region. I was hoping for words of reassurance. That the US government would surely take care of young people who came to serve in remote areas of Africa. Maybe even send in State Department staff to check on their safety.

Instead a very cold voice informed me: "Well, we keep volunteers on site even during genocidal slaughter."

"What?"

Some weeks later, after that callous comment, Belgian Army paratroopers went to Mark's village to evacuate him. So the situation was far worse than was portrayed. Unfortunately, the Congo has experienced great unrest and violence since then.

At the height of the danger to Mark, I experienced a radical shift of perspective. Some feminists call this the "click," which is when something is said or done that causes you to see your oppression up close. All looks different after that. The click happened when in desperation I confided to an aunt how concerned I was that Mark was in danger. Her only son had been in the Congo in the State Department years before, so I thought she would commiserate with me, which no one else had been able to do. Or at least offer some advice and encouragement. I guess she did, in her own way.

"Oh, Linda, you just have to pray to Our Lady. Go to Mass every day and offer it up."

That was it! I thought, *Is that all you have to offer?* Of course I had followed this model all along in my life. Prayer and offering it up to Jesus. As our nuns told us in high school and college, Jesus suffered for our sins. So we should offer up our own sufferings, pale as they are in comparison to his. But this time the advice to pray touched a deep well of anger. Is that all the Church has to offer?

The model for women in the Church is one of invisibility and silence. Till this day, women in the Catholic Church have no positions of power. That "click" made a huge difference in how I saw the Church of my youth and my place in it. I felt my anger grow, and I stayed that way for a long time. Not at my aunt but at a Church that had imposed this model of a passive Mother as the feminine God Spirit. Since I had been such a staunch Catholic, this was a huge change for me. I knew I could never go back to the old way of being.

Certainly today many people do not have any allegiance to an organized religion. But, again, that was not always so. Our family, our friends, even our neighborhood, was Catholic. It was the air we breathed. Though I knew I was not particularly saintly, I felt tied to the Catholic Church. From the black-robed Mercy nuns in elementary school who smacked my knuckles with rulers, to Grandma's sepia paintings of suffering Jesus, to the crucifixes on the walls of my childhood home, to the rituals that marked the seasons. Then the religion of my family was expanded and deepened with four years of college theology. Afterwards, I actually read theology and religion books as leisure pursuits! It was such a deep part of me.

So when that click came, it was an unraveling. Sometimes I returned to weekly Mass, but it all still felt different. As in a divorce, I have been angry, guilty, sad—yes, very sad. In any long life things change. Friends leave, children move away, even marriages disappear. Faith, however, was one aspect of my life I thought would never change.

I began to stay home from Mass, shivering at my desk alone, sure God would punish me or my husband would divorce me. We had lots of discussions about this. Yes, we had some debates, but I had to be honest about my feelings. I started attending services at other churches. But shivering alone at my desk seemed preferable. It felt like the earth had shifted under me. Eventually the anger dissipated, but that feminist click has stayed clicked.

In the few years Christopher was home after college, he and I talked a great deal about finding one's purpose in life. In being true to yourself. Though I think we'd always been close as a mom and son, at that time we actually became adult friends. He was changing, and so was I. The rock of my youth, my Catholic faith, was shattering under my feet. I was a mom without children at home, so that role was gone. Teaching was limited in its room for growth, especially in a city district not interested in change. Christopher and I talked about growth a great deal. It laid the groundwork for many transitions for us both. He was trying to decide what his next step would be, and it seemed that step was going to be far from his Buffalo home.

When he moved into an apartment in 1991, he would actually call to ask if I wanted to go out for coffee. Sometimes we met for lunch at our favorite Greek restaurant. I was actually surprised and pleased that he seemed interested in what I thought. In addition, he went out with Bob and me for dinners to our favorite Italian restaurant. We all three talked over pasta and wine. It seemed a time of deeper family relations.

I began taking courses for a second Master's degree at the University of Buffalo, purportedly to help my teaching, but mostly to grow personally. That was harder to say. Sure, I rebelled against starched tablecloths and dinner on the table at five o'clock. But I kept family as my central concern. In my bones I wanted the close relationship with my sons that I had with my parents. With Mark literally off my personal map and Christopher heading to Seattle, I needed to find a new route for myself.

Writing poetry, to my surprise, became a creative outlet. A wonderful program at Canisius College in the summer of 1987 helped me find my words. I even sent my early poems to Mark and Christopher. They both encouraged me. To improve my writing I took a poetry course from a famous poet. There I was, almost fifty years old, in a class with college kids. The first time I read a poem to the class, my heart was beating so loudly I was sure everyone could hear it. The famous poet did not like it. Strangely, or perhaps not, he did not like most poems written by women students. Instead of offering us his insights in response to our work, he just dismissed it. When one poor woman read a deeply felt poem about the death of her father, he laughed! I was appalled. I stopped attending class, something I had never done before.

One day on campus, when I actually attended the class at the end of the semester to turn in my final paper, I ran into a women's studies professor I knew from a workshop years before. Ruth and I chatted. I told her about The Poet.

"Why not come to our department?" she asked. "You can take the Intro to Women's Studies course, and we will do an independent study where you do a paper on a topic of your choice for graduate credit."

That was amazing. A professor and a department that would support me. So I began taking one course at a time. I began to discover amazing women writers who articulated theories that connected deeply with my life experience.

The seventies saw the most exciting books written by women thinkers: Kate Millett's *Sexual Politics*, Phyllis Chesler's *Women and Madness*, and Mary Daly's *Beyond God the Father*. But I did not discover them until the nineties. Reading them in my women's studies classes and studying them in addition to other theorists like Adrienne Rich and Audre Lorde, who were also poets, felt exciting. As if I were seeing something for the first time. These writers were connecting in a deep way. I now saw my mother, and us her daughters, as having been formed by our patriarchal world. The stories my mother told me about women in our family who had been abused by husbands made more sense. There was a shock of recognition, another "click." Even before I knew Christopher was gay, I learned about the parallels between discrimination against women and against LGBTQ persons.

The major historical movements of the later part of the twentieth century have influenced both Christopher and me: gay rights and second-wave feminism. I came late to the feminist party, and, as a Catholic woman raised in the fifties, I found it harder to shed some of the rules of that world.

A few years later, I earned a Master's degree in Humanities. Then I found myself at a crossroads. Did I want to continue in a Ph.D. program? If I were serious about it, I'd need to focus on my studies. I talked to the director of the English Department in the Buffalo Public Schools. The only option was an unpaid leave. It was a frightening decision for both Bob and me. But there was this deep-seated need for change, even though the loss of pay for that year was hard for us.

From our talks Christopher knew I was looking for something new in my life. In our frequent phone conversations, he really listened to my anxiety about the changes I was making. I kept saying to him that I would be pushing sixty when I finished.

"Well, you would be pushing sixty with or without the degree."

I persisted because Bob, Christopher, and Mark encouraged me. In the women's studies department, I found my way to a new path, a journey to a Ph.D. That beginning led to a degree in American Studies with a focus on women's studies and education.

When I finally walked down the aisle at the U.B. Center for the Arts to receive my Ph.D. in 2002, Christopher sent a note of congratulations: "I remember the conversations, the phone calls, when you wondered why.... And though there may have been rocky times, the years were filled with discovery."

Despite my initial self doubt, my doctorate led to a teaching job at SUNY Buffalo State College for almost nine years. That was definitely a position I loved. It enabled me to share with future teachers what I learned about teaching, my hard-won lessons begun back at East High School. Maybe all the angst was worth it. Maybe as Czeslaw Milosz says, "Who serves best doesn't always understand."

Chapter 12
Christopher: Heading West

Go West, young man, go West and grow up with the country.
—Horace Greeley, New York Tribune, 1865

Hope springs eternal and all that, yet isn't it a fact that when we give up and quit hoping; genuinely, sincerely quit hoping, things usually change for the better?
—Tom Robbins, Skinny Legs and All

In the late summer of 1993, I packed all my worldly possessions—clothes, some books, a well-played Indigo Girls cassette tape, a small tent—into my sky-blue Hyundai hatchback, kissed my parents goodbye, and drove away from my childhood home. While Mom was almost certainly crying her eyes out, I hopped on I-90 just outside of Buffalo and headed west. My destination was as far away as the interstate could take me.

I had never been to Seattle before, but a friend who had lived there for several years spoke glowingly of its mountains and water and laid-back vibe. Briefly, I contemplated going east instead, dreaming of a life as an aspiring actor in New York. The national press had just started to turn its attention to Seattle, though, and, aside from coffee, grunge, and green, the regional theaters were getting lots of positive press.

Although the farthest from home I had ever lived was Cleveland, the West Coast seemed close compared to central Africa, where Mark had spent two years in the Peace Corps. I was twenty-five and had no career to speak of. Besides, I like coffee.

I headed west.

Back at the start of that summer, still in Buffalo, I was cast in the ensemble of *Romeo & Juliet* at Shakespeare in Delaware Park. My hair newly grown long, I fancied myself a young Elizabethan noble. I spent most nights after performances at Ray Flynn's bar drinking Jameson with the cast and most days planning my journey.

I was seeing a therapist named Lou at the time, having started counseling sessions after my struggles with suicidal thoughts in the spring. I made the decision to avoid telling Lou about my sexual attraction to men. Instead, I spent our sessions explaining how I was sure I needed to find a path to follow in life. Confidence. Surety. Happiness. Those were the things I wanted. Somewhere there was a roadmap to manhood that I had missed growing up. Once I had that, I was certain other aspects of life would settle into place. All it would take was some help gathering my bearings and plotting a new course, a bit of redirection perhaps, and soon I, too, would be married with kids, just like a few friends from college who had already met that milestone. I kept pushing for an answer from Lou, a middle-aged man I looked up to as a wise older brother. He was reluctant to provide me with one.

"Christopher, you're young," he said. "Remain open. Don't block yourself off from anything. You gain confidence by doing things, not by telling yourself to be confident."

I wasn't used to this kind of advice from someone in authority. I expected to be told exactly what to do, expected the rules to be laid out for me. Dr. Roger had been very clear and direct in what I needed to do to subvert my attraction to men. Lou's encouragement to follow my own instincts was the opposite of everything I had experienced before—from school, my parents. From the church.

I took his advice as tacit approval of my plan to leave Buffalo and see what Seattle had to offer. I wanted a change, wanted to, as Lou said, do something. In the face of protests about going so far away from Mom and Dad and my grandparents and my friends, Lou's words were all the encouragement I needed.

Packing my things involved cleaning out the closet in my childhood bedroom. One evening when my parents were out, I lit a small charcoal fire in the grill out back. Once the coals were glowing red, I piled on the torn pages of all the journals I had kept since childhood. The pages going up in smoke detailed my eighth-grade crush on Jennifer and my high school infatuation with Debra. They also contained secrets I had never told anyone: the fear I felt when Daniel kissed me in high school; my obsession with my very handsome—and very straight—friend Eric; the shame I felt after leaving a bar in college to make out with a super-hot guy I had just met.

Flames licked the edges of stark white pages with deep, flowery blue ink. Here was my sorrow at losing Karen when I studied abroad during my junior year in college. There was a snippet of the freedom I felt a couple of years before, when I first started dating Neil. I watched as fragments tinged with soot fluttered against the red and purple twilight.

For several terrified moments, I was convinced that, in this act, I was actually publishing the various scenes of my young adult love life to our neighborhood. I was certain a neighbor would catch a glimpse of my secrets, find a scrap in the yard, and think, *Well, isn't this interesting? What is this all about?* I was confident the adults who watched me grow up for years and years would suddenly have all their wonderings about me confirmed.

The fire died down, the pages disappeared, and my secrets safely turned to ash. *I am free of all that past*, I thought. *I am casting a new role for myself.* I was determined to leave Buffalo and start fresh, unhampered by memories of late-night conversations in the family room and visits to those bars in Allentown. I would finally liberate myself from the desires for this classmate or that neighbor. I could burn it all away. Be done with it. Have it gone from my life.

Escaping from Buffalo and pursuing acting in Seattle felt exactly like the kind of fresh start I needed to help me figure out my life. With the windows cranked down, I sped through states I'd never visited before, letting the wind blow my hair while I sang at the top of my lungs about taking my life less seriously. Seattle appeared as a mirage on the horizon, strange and green and blue and absolutely beautiful.

As a new arrival to Seattle in the fall of 1993, I was drinking it all in. Kurt Cobain and Eddie Vedder sang about my angst and restlessness and the search for freedom I had been pursuing so relentlessly. I grew my hair even longer, wore flannel shirts from the Chicken Soup Brigade's thrift shop on Capitol Hill and was cast in plays that performed in a church basement and no one ever came to see.

In the Beginning was my first Seattle acting gig. Our cast of eight dressed all in black used rain sticks, masks, and scarves to present creation stories from a variety of cultures. In one touching scene, I knelt on the floor, gently fluttering a blue silk scarf that became, through the magic of the theater, the vast waters covering Mother Earth. Performing one night for our largest crowd yet— there were seven in the audience—I felt such a hole inside. Was this why I had packed all my earthy belongings in a car and traveled west? What the hell was I doing here in this church hall, so far from home, so far from those I loved and all that I knew? This was the new life I hoped for? *This*?

During the day, I worked as a bike messenger. Through Seattle's dampest, most depressing months, I delivered architectural plans, legal briefs, and all kinds of documents needing signatures to and from offices throughout the city. It was a job that only a few years later, as the internet grew, became obsolete.

One of my own frequent stops was at a coffee cart on Stewart and Eighth across from the old Greyhound station. Shawn was the barista, and his charm and intelligence won me over immediately. He cracked jokes and smiled in a bashful yet adorable way. He was able to hold forth on any variety of topical issues of the day. We bonded over our crummy jobs and our desire to live creative, free-spirited lives. I invited him to have drinks one night with some actor friends at the Deluxe on Broadway. He charmed them as well.

When I wasn't dreaming of the meatloaf sandwich I would eat for lunch or the steak I would broil for dinner in my basement room in Queen Anne, I found myself thinking of Shawn. He was handsome, in an unwashed, grungy sort of way. Tall and lean, he had long, wavy hair and a goatee. And those eyes. Eyes so dreamy it was easy to overlook that he had a sometimes boyfriend in Bellingham. Eyes so beautiful it was easy to forget that I was not attracted to men.

Wait. I *was* attracted to men. I was incredibly attracted to Shawn, just as I had been attracted to Neil and Eric and men in general for as long as I could remember. So what if I happened to have another fling with a guy? Would that be so terrible? Maybe I was bisexual. Maybe I shouldn't cut myself off from this experience. What was the worst thing that could happen?

In the middle of all this, I flew home to Buffalo for Christmas. I spent time with my family and even visited Caitlin. Dad thought I seemed depressed after seeing her and delicately suggested that perhaps I should consider getting back together with her and returning to Buffalo. Before I left, Mom and I discussed my plans to return to Buffalo in March for my grandfather's eightieth birthday. On my way back to Seattle, I stopped for a few days in Chicago to visit Eileen, a friend from college. She had just given birth to her first child, a child conceived out of wedlock with a guy she'd met in the Peace Corps.

Eileen is one of six children from a conservative, Irish Catholic family. Her parents were furious with her for getting pregnant and deciding to have the baby without getting married first. Crammed into her apartment, I held her baby and listened as she spoke with her typical passion about falling in love and doing what she knew to be right. It was her life, she reasoned. There was nobody—parents, the church, the baby's father—who could tell her that this beautiful child was anything less than exactly what life was supposed to be about, husband or not.

I came clean about my own transgression. "I think I might be attracted to guys," I told her.

"Okay," she said.

"It doesn't feel okay."

"You're a great guy, Draj. If you're gay, so what? Nothing's going to change the way we feel about you. We'll still love you."

She smiled. I smiled. "Thanks. I needed that."

I left Chicago and headed back to Seattle clearer about the path ahead. If Eileen's family could learn to accept her and love her beautiful baby, maybe there was hope for my family. If she could persevere, I could, too. I was twenty-five, and it was becoming clear that I wasn't going to stop dreaming about men. Instead of the miraculous change I had envisioned when I drove away from Buffalo, I was traveling a road that wasn't leading me anywhere different.

Up to that point, my life was this thing that existed outside of me, a game to play, a puzzle to figure out, something that required work in order to navigate. It was a destination, not a road. I had approached my life as something I could fix or shape, not something I lived in. Now, though, I started to see Lou's encouragement about staying open in a new light. The path was right there in front of me, or if not in front, then inside of me, just as much a part of me as it had been for as long as I could remember. I thought about Eileen and knew that there were those who would love me just as I was. I thought about Shawn, and how touching him and kissing him and being with him made me feel. I thought about what it meant to sin and felt that, regardless of what priests and teachers and even the Bible might say, they had to be wrong. They were wrong.

The only thing to do was be open to my life as it was, accept it and then see what it could be.

Spring comes early in Seattle, especially if you grew up with snow that often lasted through March and into April. I was startled to see trees budding before the final days of February and was sure that something was very wrong. The spring rain was still a hassle for my courier job, but now I had something else to focus on. I was spending more and more time with Shawn, including nights at his apartment on Capitol Hill. Just as it had three years before in Buffalo, that spring seemed to bloom and bloom around me with wonder and possibility. With light.

I shared my secret with a few new friends, and they nodded, gave me a hug, and said, in essence, "That's nice." Then we went on discussing politics, or our recent auditions, or whatever. It was no big deal in liberal 1994 Seattle to be gay, and that blew my mind. I didn't need to discuss the intimate details of when and how and why with anyone. I owed nobody an explanation about anything. Nobody expected one. I wanted my sexual orientation to be an aspect of me, one quality of many. It was important that it didn't completely define me. In Seattle it didn't.

But Seattle wasn't Buffalo, friends are not family, and I was no fool. I knew that when men came out to their parents, the anger and shock those parents felt often led to a child being cut off, even kicked out, and disowned. I had no reason to believe that my parents would react like that. I trusted their compassion and open-mindedness. On the other hand, I had never heard them discuss gay people in a positive way. I had rarely heard them discuss gay people at all. There was a chance that anger, fear, and a lack of knowledge could fuel an emotional reaction on their part. I believed they loved me. I trusted that nothing could ever change that. But, still, I was scared as hell to come out to them.

I was going back to Buffalo in March for my grandfather's birthday, and a few weeks before that I found a copy of *Beyond Acceptance: Parents of Lesbians and Gays Talk About Their Experiences* at Beyond the Closet Bookstore on Capitol Hill. In those pages, which I quickly devoured, parents were sharing their perspective on what it was like to find out that their child was gay. They articulated the pain, fear, and challenges they faced when confronted with a new truth about someone they had known since birth. But the stories didn't end there. Again and again, parents wrote about how they came around to understanding, acceptance, and change.

I couldn't believe what I was reading. Somewhere in this world, in this very country, there were parents—many of them, in fact—who had found a way to move past their initial discomfort, learn something they had never thought they would have to learn, and to continue loving their children. One parent in the book said, "When I found out Don was gay, it was hard certainly. But a day or two after I knew, I was sitting by myself and thought 'He's still the same son who asked me for five dollars this morning; he's the same boy who was here for breakfast, who took out the trash, who wrecked the car. His sexuality doesn't have anything to do with his integrity or his ability to love or his worth.' He's a loving, honest, and wonderful son. He told me he's gay, and he's still a loving, honest, and wonderful son." It was passages like this, in their plain, humble, everyday eloquence, that I could imagine my own parents thinking and saying.

I decided I would come out to my parents during the visit to Buffalo for my grandfather's birthday party. I wanted to have a face-to-face conversation with them and didn't want to wait any longer before having it. The visit would be short, and there were a variety of activities planned, including a birthday dinner for thirty people at an Italian restaurant hosted by Mom and my aunt. Looking back, I can see that Mom must have had a thousand last-minute details to iron out and that the afternoon of the party was probably not the best time to come out. At the time, all I knew was that I wanted to get the task accomplished.

Mark was living in Washington, D.C. at the time, and he, too, was home for the party. Because he is my brother and one of my closest friends and because I trust his judgment and needed his validation, I had shared some of my confusion a few years earlier. A few weeks before the party, I had come out to him over the phone.

"It just doesn't matter here," I boasted.

I sensed in his response the slightest bit of hesitation. I'm pretty sure he said that he couldn't quite bring himself to say that it didn't matter. But I didn't press. Was that his own grief? His concern that we might not have kids and be uncles together? Was there homophobia?

He did say that he loved me no matter what. And that he was sure our parents would feel the same way.

I told Mark I would be coming out to Mom and Dad on the day of the party. As I was getting ready to go to lunch with Dad, Mark nodded from behind his coffee and gave me a look of relief and expectation.

"Good luck," he said. "I'm glad I don't have to do it."

It was important to me that I have a separate discussion with each of my parents. I wanted each of them to have their own reactions. I didn't want Mom to feel like she had to take care of Dad. I wanted Dad to be honest and interact with me and not yield all the emotional heavy lifting to Mom. I had no idea what I was going to say, and in the car on the way to lunch I was running possible scripts through my head.

"I'm still the same person. You just know a more complete version of who I am."

"I have always been this way, and it's certainly nothing you or Mom did to make me like this."

"There's this sex researcher named Alfred Kinsey who talks about a scale of sexual attraction. A zero on his scale is completely heterosexual, and a seven is completely homosexual. I'm somewhere around a six."

Talking with straight guys about sex had always been like speaking a foreign language to me. It wasn't just that I lacked an understanding of idiomatic phrases, or that I wasn't confident about pronunciation. All of that was problematic, to be sure. More than that, I was deficient when it came to basic vocabulary, syntax, and perhaps most importantly, attitude. I would sit on the sidelines of conversations that veered towards sexual conquests and swagger, planning in vain what I might say. I laughed too loud in the wrong places. I stuttered and sweated. I sat, terrified and mute, in awe as the beautiful, arrogant, childlike banter unfolded.

Dad never talked in any disparaging way about women. He is not one to brag about anything. He would certainly never objectify a woman. That said, he also was not one to talk about sex at all. The last conversation I recalled having about sex was when I was twelve and he and Mom drew a few crude diagrams and explained human reproduction to me and Mark. In this conversation we were about to have, Dad and I would both be strangers in a strange land. I didn't want to be talking about sex with Dad. That was just odd. Now I would have to find the language to discuss my attraction to men, something I never expected to say, something I was sure he never expected to hear.

We sat in the Towne Restaurant and made our way through small talk over chicken souvlaki sandwiches. Dad asked, as he always did, how I was doing financially. Did I need any money?

The bill came, and it was time. Now or never.

"Dad, I'm gay."

There was a slight pause. I noticed that quick shake of his head that my father does when he's surprised by something. He looked away, out the window. Then, he turned to me. We locked eyes for a brief moment, and I was the one to turn away.

I had no idea how to fully communicate everything I wanted to say. That it wasn't something I could change, although I had tried. That I was still me. That, more than anything, I just needed him to love me.

"Son," he said, "I love you no matter what."

He sniffed, then blew his nose quickly into his napkin. I muttered something about Kinsey and his scale, no doubt completely confusing him, and he indicated that it was probably time to go. We drove home, as I recall, entirely in silence.

Mark was drinking coffee and reading the paper at the kitchen table when we returned. Dad hurried upstairs to shower and shave and probably try to figure out the extent to which his life had just changed. Mark and I exchanged a nod, a look.

"How did it go?"

"Fine. I think."

"You going to tell Mom?"

"Yup."

"Now?"

"Yes. Now."

Mom and I went to a coffee shop we had frequented during the years I lived in Buffalo after college. Snow swirled outside the windows and steam rose from our mugs. It felt so similar to the dozens of times we had been here before. Everything afterward would be different.

"Mom, I'm gay."

The first thing I remember her saying was "Just promise me one thing. Promise me you will have kids." I think I laughed and said, "I just told you I'm gay. That's the first thing you have to say?"

Years later, Mom recalled it differently. "I was grieving," she said. "I always thought you would make such a great father, but I was worried that was not going to be an option for you anymore. What did I know? I didn't know many gay people, and certainly none with kids."

Grandpa's party happened. He was eighty and his eyes sparkled and he had a bit too much to drink and everyone told him what a great guy he was because it was true. The conversations at dinner were the same as they often were. Friends and family wanted to know how I liked living in Seattle and when I would be home next. I felt free and light that evening, toasting Pa and eating Italian food, but it seemed strange, too. Mom, Dad, and Mark knew my secret. Nothing had changed. Everything had changed.

The next night Mom cooked a big dinner for the family. Right before the meal came to the table, while Aunt Judy was in the kitchen and we grandkids were chatting in the living room with our grandparents, there was a loud crash in the kitchen. Mom had dropped a platter and smashed it.

"Linda, are you okay? What's wrong?" my aunt asked.

I couldn't hear Mom's reply, and my imagination ran wild. I worried that she was rattled by my confession in the coffee shop and that our conversation the previous day was not reflective of her true feelings. I was certain that now, in hushed tones, she was explaining to her sister her sadness or worry or anger. I was terrified about what was still unsaid between us.

I retreated to Seattle the next day, tucked myself into my tiny basement apartment, found safety in Shawn's arms, and, at some point over the next few days, I cried like I hadn't since I was a baby. Something inside had asserted itself, was no longer willing to be silenced, and finally, finally, I let go. The hope and the pretending I had carefully packed and lugged around with me I ditched for good. In sharing this truth with those I loved most, life seemed unbearably light.

These were tears of relief. No longer having to hide or pretend, I would find over the next days and weeks and months a new spaciousness in my Seattle life. I no longer worried about mannerisms or modulating my voice. I didn't care about where my gaze might fall. Instead, I felt free to look if a handsome man met my gaze. I was no longer concerned that someone would think I was gay. I was gay, and that was that. I settled into myself. I became more confident without trying. I didn't try so hard.

But those tears were also in part generated from self-pity and fear. I was scared about what came next, not just for me but for my family as well. How had we changed? What would we become? Had I made a mistake in making my identity a public declaration?

Some gay men decided to keep it to themselves, kept their private lives private, and moved forward with their separate worlds. I knew of men who stayed closeted at work and who remained bachelors in the eyes of their family; men who dated other men, had long-term relationships even, but to colleagues, family members, and all but a close group of friends, their partners were just good friends.

That didn't sit quite well with me, and I wanted to live a more integrated, complete life. That's where the self-pity came in. I had spent a quarter of a century living in fear and denial, not working toward that shameless and integral life, and that made me want to shake my fists at God, Jesus, and Mary, the mother of God.

It is fair to say that out of the self-pity, a deep and finely pointed anger grew. At the top of the list of targets was the Catholic church. My Catholic childhood and young adulthood gave me a firm moral compass, a wealth of ritual and celebration, and a community of wonderful people who lived lives of love and generosity and care. But after coming out I was starting to peel back the layers of guilt and shame, recognizing that I had kindness and love and generosity in me, and that my sexuality was something I had not chosen and it could not be a sin. I remember thinking to myself that I didn't do drugs, wasn't violent or sexually abusive, was attentive to family and tried to help friends. I gave back to my community. I certainly wasn't perfect, but who I happened to find attractive and love couldn't be a sin. It just couldn't.

The head of the Church in the formative years of my youth was Pope John Paul II, who led the church from 1978 until his death in

2005. Although he recognized the dignity and rights of homosexual individuals, under his watch the catechism maintained that homosexual activity was a sin. He preached that even HIV-positive individuals should not use condoms while having sex. When some European nations started to discuss allowing same-sex couples to enter into civil unions, he wrote that this was "perhaps part of a new ideology of evil." The Church, which I had learned was supposed to be the embodiment of Jesus Christ's message to love your neighbor, seemed to be, under the pope's leadership, very selective about which neighbors deserved that love.

Those who were representatives of the church did not seem any better. Fr. Edmeston, my parish priest at St. Rose, never spoke of the inherent dignity and rights of homosexuals from the pulpit. Of all the Christian Brothers at St. Joe's, all the Jesuits at John Carroll, and all the lay teachers who taught us religious education, I can only recall one who ever taught us anything positive or worthy about homosexuals. If any of them reprimanded or punished students who called me and my friends "faggot" or "homo" or any of a wide variety of other slurs, it failed to make a lasting impression.

Catholic family members and close friends were complicit, often looking the other way or joining in when jokes were made to denigrate homosexuals. Relatives mocked gay people at family gatherings. A neighbor thought it was funny to have his photo taken with his wife's purse and a limp wrist. The list goes on and on. It's depressing to think about, and I try not to spend too much time remembering. My life would have been so much better if these adults—and many more—had taken a moment to think about the harm they were causing with their words, their actions and inactions, their power and influence.

Of course, the Catholic church did not have a corner on the market of intolerance. Condemnation of homosexual orientation and behavior by religious groups seemed so pervasive when I was growing up that it was the rare exception of acceptance—say, from the Unitarian Church—that seemed extraordinary. The messages that my friends and I heard in the 1980s from the likes of Pat Robertson, Jerry Falwell, and James Dobson continued for decades, with more and more preachers using homosexuality as a tool to prey on the ignorance of their followers and anyone who would listen, continuing to sow hatred and fear.

The Reverend Fred Phelps of the Westboro Baptist Church was one of these purveyors of hate. In 1998, Phelps led his congregation in picketing the funeral of Matthew Shepard, a young man from Laramie, Wyoming, who was beaten to death by two men, allegedly because of his homosexuality. Similar picketing has continued for years at funerals for celebrities, religious leaders, and service members killed in the line of duty all because of Westboro's belief that society's tolerance and acceptance of homosexuality is inviting God's anger and wrath upon us.

Elected officials and political activists did their fair share of damage as well. In 1977, after a local ordinance in Dade County, Florida prohibited discrimination on the basis of sexual orientation, Anita Bryant ran the "Save Our Children" campaign to repeal the ordinance. This made her a public symbol of homophobia and bigotry to some, but to others she was a hero. In 1978, Dan White, a member of the San Francisco Board of Supervisors, killed San Francisco Mayor George Moscone and Supervisor Harvey Milk. Milk was the first openly gay elected official in California and would have undoubtedly continued his courageous and uncompromising leadership in the LGBTQ community. White was found guilty of voluntary manslaughter and not murder because his lawyers effectively argued, in what became known as the "Twinkie defense," that he had a diminished capacity because he had eaten too much junk food in the hours before the attack.

In 1981, the same year the first deaths from AIDS were reported in the *New York Times,* Ronald Reagan became president of the United States. Reagan pretty much ignored the AIDS crisis, and the deaths of almost an entire generation of gay men occurred on his watch. In 1993, less than a year before I came out, President Bill Clinton proposed the "Don't Ask, Don't Tell" policy, which allowed homosexual and bisexual persons to serve in the military as long as they kept their sexuality a secret. The policy did little to end the practice of discharging service members because of their sexual orientation and only encouraged more dishonesty and fear among gay and bisexual servicemembers.

Once I was a confirmed member of the LGBTQ community, I could no longer pretend that these people, these institutions, were not hurting me. I read everything I could about the history of persecution and harassment directed toward gays and lesbians. I subscribed to *The Advocate,* a national monthly LGBTQ news magazine, and read each issue cover to cover for years. I watched movies with gay themes and characters when I could find them.

I read biographies and autobiographies of famous gay men, and attended pride parades each June. Newly educated, my anger only seemed to increase. Instead of feeling pride and acceptance, I was pissed. How could we, humans just like me, be treated so horribly? Why was the simple matter of who we were attracted to such a threat to anyone?

Not long after I came out, I found out that, during the year we were seeing him for counseling, Dr. Roger told my parents in a private session that I was dealing with issues related to my sexual orientation, but that he was confident everything would "work out all right." I was stunned when Mom told me this.

"But he said that the information I was sharing with him was just between him and me."

"I know."

"He promised that he wasn't sharing anything I said with you."

"I know."

Fuck him, I thought.

He had broken the trust I'd placed in him by sharing my struggles with Mom and Dad. Not only that, but his horrible advice to try to change my sexual arousal pattern contributed to years of denial and false hope. I have often considered writing him a letter and laying it all on the line. "How could you?" I imagine myself writing. "Do you know the damage you did? I'm better now, no thanks to you."

I have also thought about reporting him for malpractice. He had hurt me with his bad advice, and I wanted him to pay. I wanted to prevent others from ending up with the same bogus advice

I had received. I told the story of what he'd done to as many of my friends as possible over the years, and secretly delighted in their shock and horror at his behavior.

It is hard to write these words, but those closest to me deserved some of my anger as well. Mom and Dad could have done more. They should have done more. What if we had more honesty and fewer secrets? Why hadn't they created an atmosphere where telling them my secret wouldn't be such a big deal? Why was the burden on me to tell them this thing when they were the ones who had chosen a religion that was so hateful and paternalistic toward gay men and women? What would my life have been like if they just confronted me at some point and asked if I was gay? Why didn't they come to me when Dr. Roger told them I was struggling with my sexual orientation? That could have been positive, to have it all out in the open. Parents are often counseled not to ask a child if they are gay because it can be damaging to self-esteem if they are not. But it was damaging for me, while I struggled alone, to go unrecognized.

A week or two after I returned to Seattle from Buffalo, as my new life unfolded with Shawn, the first letter from my parents arrived. Over the next few months, we wrote back and forth. Together, the distance between us and ancient art of letter writing smoothed over warranted and unwarranted fears on both our parts.

"Your mother and I talked. We love you. I told my friend Ron."

"You did the best you could. Have you heard of PFLAG?" Started by the mother of a gay man in 1973, this support group was often the first place parents went after their children came out. I knew my parents would find comfort there.

"Promise me you will have kids." Again, this line from Mom.

Each mail delivery brought with it a sense of relief, and I found it easier to communicate my love and worry and sameness through my replies. Writing afforded me the opportunity to share some of the passages I had read in *Beyond Acceptance*, and they looked compelling and honest and real on the page.

That June, I returned to Buffalo for a summer visit. The hint of reservation or hesitation or distance that had crept in between Dad and me after my visit in March was gone. After asking about my finances, he talked about feeling confident that there was nothing about me that should be hidden from anyone. Mom spoke about the books she was reading, the PFLAG meeting she and Dad attended, and my bravery.

There's a passage in *Beyond Acceptance* that I love:

"Sooner or later [...] parents have to go beyond the cultural messages of rejection and hatred if they are to feel any peace. Facing the problem may cost us a great deal of time and pain. It is frightening to let go of established guideposts when there are only shaky and unproven ones to replace them. And there may be little help from any of the traditional sources such as church, social groups, extended family, or even close friends. Parents must sink or swim by their own efforts.

"But swim many of them do."

Mom and Dad are definitely swimmers.

Opinion

Front Page > Opinion > Everybody's Column

Email | Print | Most Popular | Headlines by Email

Previous | Next

Gays deserve the dignity of marriage

8/19/2003

One of the best things about Buffalo is our community values based on tight-knit families and friends who become like family. My husband and I are part of such a close community. Our children were raised with lots of interactions with family and friends.

Now our grown children have moved away and started their own families. One of our sons happens to be gay. Reading in yesterday's Buffalo News that President Bush will work to prevent my son from ever aspiring to a legal committed relationship with all the ordinary human dignity and family values he knew as a child grieves me. My son is a wonderful teacher, a responsible citizen, a loving son, and a committed life partner for more than three years.

The current de[...]
freedom: to lov[...]
"conservative"[...]

It is a double g[...]
work feverishly[...]
so children of [...]
promoted by J[...]
beloved son a[...]
all that is Chris[...]

That such edu[...]
Senate Majorit[...]
in our country [...]
are denied bec[...]
hospital visitati[...]

These leaders [...]
unnatural way [...]
heterosexual h[...]
orientation as [...]
choose.

I want him to h[...]
person he love[...]
human desires[...]
happiness." It [...]

LINDA DRAJM[...]
Buffalo

Chapter 13
Linda: Coming Out for a Mom

Oh son,
Know that the psyche has its own
Fame, whether known or not that
Soul can flame like feathers of a bird.
Grow into your own plumage, brightly,
So that any tree is a marvelous city.
—James Applewhite, "Prayer for My Son"

For my father's eightieth birthday on a cold wintry March day, Christopher was visiting from Seattle. It was so good to have him home. He asked me to go out for coffee, and of course I agreed quickly. Before he'd left for Seattle, we used to go out for coffee or tea on occasion and just talk about life. So this seemed like a good way to connect to that earlier time we'd developed an adult friendship and moved beyond the mother-son conflicts of the teen years.

Now he was twenty-five years old and living out his dream of being an actor in Seattle. Around us in the coffee house, people took off their heavy winter coats and raised steaming cups of coffee. The air smelled of damp boots, coffee, and baking scones. On that Saturday, the restaurant was packed. I even saw some friends across the room eating pancakes. I wanted to take Christopher over to meet them. But he stopped me and said we had to talk. As we nestled into a cozy booth, I noticed a different feel in the atmosphere. What came next changed everything.

"Mom, I need to tell you something."

"Okay. I'm glad we have time to talk with all the stuff going on about Pa's party."

"I am gay."

That was a message I did not expect to hear. I mumbled something about how he must have struggled with this issue. Though I was shaken, we talked in the open way we had developed in the previous year before his move. I was so glad we had developed this adult ease in communicating. He told me he had already told his dad and his brother. Most importantly, he said he did not want to hide such an important part of himself from us. Best of all, he said we could continue to talk even after he returned to Seattle, and he welcomed my questions and concerns.

As we slowly made our way out, we stood outside in the cold Buffalo winter and continued talking. Piles of snow rose on the sidewalks. Flakes swirled around our heads. Heedless, we just kept talking. I felt if we just kept talking it would somehow all feel right. It was then I said I was sad that he would not become a dad, that I thought he would be a great dad. And I added with emphasis, " Besides, I want grandchildren."

To my surprise, he laughed, actually laughed. Somehow that really cheered me.

"Well, maybe it will happen. You never know."

I have to say I totally doubted him. It was a good way to end the conversation, but getting through the rest of the weekend was a challenge. I had my dad's birthday party to navigate. A big gathering at a local restaurant. There was no time to really process my feelings in response to what Christopher had just said. I just felt shocked and, I guess, fearful. Family was the big issue for me. Would I lose my beloved son to a lifestyle I could not really imagine just then? Outside of seeing gay men in parades wearing drag or lots of leather, my contact with gay life was minimal. I had lots of worries and questions. Was he going to get AIDS? Would he still want to be close to the family? Was his lifestyle going to radically change? At the same time, I felt so guilty that he had struggled for so long and that we, his parents, were not there to help or at least reassure him of our love.

Certainly I knew gay people, of course. A lesbian couple were close friends. One of the women was a wonderful writer/teacher who started the writing group of which I was a member. But I knew only one gay man, a colleague at my school, and he certainly did not have children. I did not think family would be possible for my Christopher. My wonderful son with such a capacity for generous love would be a lonely gay man prone to nightclubbing and marching in gay rights parades wearing leather or drag.

At the time I never really considered that my son was gay, a term I did not use then. I knew Christopher did not fit the macho model of heterosexual males, all into athletics, but as a teacher I had male colleagues who did not fit that stereotype either. My closest friend at the high school where I taught did not watch football games on Sundays, but attended the Buffalo Philharmonic classical series. He was a happily married man and father to three boys. My strong belief at the time, one I often preached to my students, was that stereotypes may hurt others, and we must try to avoid them at all costs. That was a message I tried to attend to as well, not always successfully.

I was happy when Christopher was in plays at his high school. I loved theater myself and loved sharing that with him. When he was in high school, I saw his participation in plays as a sign of an artistic temperament, which I valued. Living with my husband and older son who were both so consumed with sports, I thought it was great to have a family member in the arts. Wrongly, as it turned out, I believed that the school encouraged all its students in a wide variety of interests and that there were no strict gender roles for young men. Only years later did I learn how much pain Christopher endured during those high school years from name-calling by the jocks.

Maybe the most powerful reason that Christopher's reality did not invade my consciousness was that we lived in an enclosed world where so-called alternative lifestyles made very little impact. It was a very straight world. We all three went to a therapist, Dr. Roger, during a particularly dark time in his senior year. Dr. Roger later told us Christopher was struggling with his sexuality but not to worry since it was just a passing phase. He also said that we should not confront Christopher with this knowledge since he needed room to process his feelings on his own. That all made sense to me. Of course in hindsight I see how misguided it was.

How shocking that he told us! And how shocking that we listened. There are so many times that parents are not sure what to do. How I wish I would have reassured Christopher that our love for him would never change. How I wish I could have offered words of comfort and support. Maybe it would have sped him on his journey to being who he is. Maybe it would have saved him from another five years of wondering and worrying, or, as Dr. Roger said, maybe it would have upset him that we knew and cause him to retreat from us and ruin our relationship.

After that, Bob and I watched him and worried. But I guess his acting skills were good. In college, he seemed self-assured. He had a beautiful girlfriend and a slew of friends from the newspaper. We thought the psychiatrist was right about his feelings as just a passing phase. As a teacher I read a great deal about adolescent psychology, and I knew teens struggled to discover who they are. The world of adults is confusing and it offers many options of ways to be. Of course adolescents go through phases, so I did not wonder too much at this diagnosis. Plus he was a psychiatrist and knew way more than me, or so I assumed.

In today's world, I cannot believe parents would fail to consider the issue with their child, that they would not ask if there were a concern about sexual identity they needed to talk about. Especially if the child seemed depressed. Just recently, I was talking to a writer friend who told me about her transgendered adult child. She said, "I'm so glad that these things are so open now." I felt a frisson of guilt.

"Oh, they were not like that twenty-five years ago," I told her, and went on to describe how my son had suffered in high school.

We agreed that things are not perfect now, but still it is so much more open nowadays.

My previous experience with young gay people was not a positive one. In the summer of 1993, before Christopher came out, I joined a friend and went to a women's writing conference at a college a few hours away from home. What I did not realize is that "women's" was code for lesbian. At the conference, I was shocked at the openly sexual gay women I encountered. Many of the young women had tattoos and piercings. This at a time when it was totally transgressive. And rare! The older lesbians were swaggering and loud in their sexuality. I was very uncomfortable. Coming from Catholic girls' schools with prim nuns and lay schoolteachers, this was new for me. Was I also homophobic? Maybe so.

Dorothy Allison, the lesbian author, was the lead presenter. She was fearless and encouraged all of us fledging writers to be fearless. Actually she kind of scared me. Her approach to writing was far different from my previous experience as a writer and a teacher. I tried to plumb deep into my past, as she instructed, and I tried to get to know the other attendees. My friend had been to this particular yearly conference before, so she was often off socializing with the other women.

Each day we had writing time. Afterward, each of us would read what we had written. One young woman read her very graphic account of incest during one of these sessions. Afterward, with some motherly comments, I tried to be supportive of her, since it seemed she was writing about herself. But she turned on me with a ferocity I had rarely seen. Maybe she thought I conflated her sexual orientation with the abuse she endured. Or maybe I reminded her of her mother! Who knows? It rattled me to the core. She even posted an open letter on the conference bulletin board publicly decrying my behavior. I was shocked and upset.

So, when Christopher told me only a year later that he is gay, I felt this immense fear rise up in me. Would he sport tattoos and piercings? Would I not be able to be motherly? Would I lose him to a new world I did not recognize? Learning this news marked a huge shift for me. I had to come to terms with a new story about my son and about myself as a mother.

Luckily, Christopher and I had many conversations on the phone and in letters after he returned to Seattle. I read a great deal and talked to gay and straight friends. One of the first things I did was to call the hotline of our local PFLAG group. I saw an ad in our local alternative paper regarding this organization's focus on the parents of gay people. I remember that first call shortly after Christopher left for Seattle. I was tentative. But the woman on the other end was so warm I felt at ease. The only other person I had told was my sister, Judy, who in her no-nonsense way said, "So what if he is gay. He is our Chris." Of course I agreed. But in those first weeks, I was hurting. And I wondered what the future would hold for our son and our family.

At the PFLAG meetings I attended, I found helpful articles and books I could borrow. What a great supportive group. Soon I joined the board and even spoke at a panel during Pride Week. My mourning lasted about a month. What ameliorated it was that Christopher was willing to talk to me and listen to my fears about his health since AIDS was not as treatable then. We wrote letters back and forth and continued to talk on the phone. His openness made it all much easier. Best of all, I saw that he did not change. No wearing leather and hanging out in bars every night. He was the same lovable guy I'd always known.

The following June, Bob and I visited him in Seattle and met his boyfriend and many of his friends, both gay and straight. We felt very comfortable with them. They reminded us of his friends from high school and college. No bikers with leather jackets and earrings talking about their nightclub experiences, but young people who talked about movies and plays, the latest book they read. Our kind of people! I knew another dimension of my son. But I did not lose the son I had raised.

Because of his bravery, I was inspired not to hide Christopher's orientation. It inspired Bob, too. We were sure others would be accepting and affirming. We were right. My sister Judy and niece Lillian were totally loving. Not that I was surprised. But it was something new in our family. In fact, they both said that if my very conservative brother-in-law were not supportive, he would be out the door! They told him as they sat at the kitchen table, expectantly waiting. Luckily for him he said, "He is my nephew and I love him." Whew! Crisis averted.

My eighty-year-old parents were accepting as well. Christopher wanted to tell them himself. My mom was proud of herself for not crying, but she also said that this did not change her love one bit. My dad was upset we had not helped Christopher when he was in high school. He said, "We are family. We should have helped him." Yes, I felt the same way. Friends were equally supportive, saying, "He is still our lovable Chris!" I don't know if he realizes how dear he is to people.

At one point around this time, I was moved to write a column for our local newspaper protesting the Catholic Church's treatment of LGBTQ people. I don't remember exactly what triggered this strong desire. I think it was that Pope John Paul II made a public comment on how gay sex was "intrinsically evil." That really rocked me. So the piece almost wrote itself. In it, I expressed so much anger at the church of my youth that I worried about getting hate mail. But I only got one piece that promised me hell. That the rest of the responses were positive surprised me. One phone call in particular. A priest I knew called me.

"This is Father Joe," he said.

"Yes," I slowly replied, sure he was going to condemn me.

"I want to compliment you on your column."

Was I ever shocked! He went on to tell me that the diocese goes after priests who try to minister to the LGBTQ community. At the church we attended, several people also complimented me. Two different women told me their sons are gay.

But the most surprising discussion I had was with a former classmate. She took me aside at a party we both attended. She told me about her older brother, whom all the nieces and nephews in the family absolutely loved. He would come to family holidays and birthday parties alone and always leave early. Everyone would beg him to stay. Saying he was tired, he insisted on leaving.

When he was on his deathbed, he called his sister and asked

her to visit him. Then he told her of his sexual orientation and of the partner who stayed home alone for all those years of family gatherings. She was shocked and very distressed. Sadly, her brother died. His partner is now part of the family celebrations. She told me how very awful this news was for her and for her children. I think it's one of the saddest stories I've ever heard.

The biggest challenge for me was telling our close neighbors, who were staunch traditional Catholics. I knew Christopher would bring home his boyfriend, and I did not want either of them to feel uncomfortable around our home with neighbors saying something insensitive, perhaps out of ignorance. If they were not accepting of my son, I could no longer have them in my life. I felt that way about anyone: friend, relative, or neighbor.

I hesitantly crossed the street to tell Marcy, one of the most conservative. One election day we shouted at each other in her hallway because she said the Democratic nominee for mayor, whose sign was on my lawn, was a baby killer!! Despite the fact that mayors had no input into social policies. We had many doctrinal and political disagreements through the years, though we stayed friends.

So, I nervously knocked on Marcy's door and went into the dark hallway that smelled of Murphy Oil Soap. If her reaction was in any way negative, I would not be able to talk to her again. Not if she said something about my dear son!

Marcy came to the kitchen door with her hands full of soapsuds. She was drying her hands as I began rather quickly to tell her I had something important to share about our family. What happened next floored me. Marcy quit drying her hands of sudsy foam from her sink and wiped her brow. I had never seen her stop housework for any reason if she was in the middle of something. She was obsessively clean about her home.

She sat down on a stair and said, "Yeah, my sister's sons are gay, too." This she had never publicly stated before.

We talked for a while and embraced when I left. Sometimes truth brings great surprises.

Chapter 14
A Letter from Mark: Facing Our Doubts

June 11, 2014

Chris,

We sat looking at each other across one lonely candle that night in 1991 when you first told me you were gay. In my memory you were a few days into your visit to my village in Zaire, and we finally had a night to ourselves to talk. The mud hut where we sat wasn't exactly spacious or inviting, but it was a sanctuary from the perplexing challenges of negotiating village life in another culture and language. Every morning we could cook coffee and pancakes over the charcoal grill.

As momentous as the occasion was, it wasn't the only memorable one from your visit. There was the trip to the isolated river where we body-surfed through rapids; the dugout canoes we took up another river in search of hippos; the rooster you decapitated; and the bike ride across the charred savannah that so dehydrated you we had to take refuge with a missionary nurse.

People ask me now whether I knew you were gay, or even had an inkling. I really didn't. But I think that's mostly because I was so wrapped up in my own thing during high school and college, I wasn't paying close attention. Your bedroom door was closed quite often, but it never clicked that something important was going on.

What exactly you said, or how you phrased it, I don't recall. What I remember now is how wrong I was then, a pattern that sadly repeated itself. What I think I said was that being gay would make your life so hard. I thought of holidays and family meals back in Buffalo and imagined that all of that would be outside your reach. It didn't seem like a family with children was possible. Having a family that would be a part our larger Buffalo clan was inconceivable.

Wrong.

Later I would counsel you not to tell our grandparents that you were gay. Keep the secret and spare them the difficulty of grappling with it.

Wrong again.

Instead, you chose a path that required much greater courage and determination. You had the chutzpah to talk through the very difficult issues of sexuality not just with your parents, but with your grandparents and other family members.

I think we could guess with great certainty that Mom and Dad would support you no matter what, but the further the circle went out, the less sure the response would be. You never disguised anything, and that was both brave and the absolute right decision.

Later, at your third wedding (hey, but they were all to the same man!), you gave a toast that talked about watching brothers and sisters, aunts and uncles falling in love, facing doubt, and then making a commitment.

You went on to say, "We could not wait until we grew up and it happened to us. We couldn't wait, and yet we did, never imagining this day, this celebration of marriage equality would happen in our lifetime."

I love that line, but I think it understates things more than a little. You weren't waiting. With each simple declaration, be it to your grandfather or to one of your classes at school, you were tweaking the universe just a bit. Chris, your decisions to celebrate your love made us all learn and grow (and realize our wrongheadedness). The universe is bending toward justice because you did it.

Love, Mark

Chapter 15
Linda: Teaching and Learning

That is what literature offers—a language powerful enough to say how it is. It isn't a hiding place. It is a finding place.
—Jeanette Winterson, *Why Be Happy When You Could be Normal*

After Christopher opened that door to his closet, I knew my teaching had to change. If he suffered silently for years, then at least a few of the students who paraded before me year after year must have suffered as well. In 1994 I was at Hutchinson Central Technical High School. There was one teacher friend I knew who was gay. Jason was not out to students, no one was in the 1990s, but he was open to the faculty, hosting parties at his large home on the lake with his partner of many years. I went to Jason to talk to him, mostly for moral support, but then I began to see we had to do something different as teachers.

Jason and I were advisors to the student government. There was a fund available for a project every year, so we decided to order books on LGBTQ themes and make them available to students for the '94-'95 school year. Jason was a biology teacher, so the plan was that I would use the books in my English classes. It's amazing how many hurdles we had to surmount for such a simple project. First, the student leaders had to be on board, which to our surprise they were. Just to be sure there would be no blowback, we had to get the principal's approval without letting the school board know. One good thing about a big city school district is that often the central administration and school board are removed from decisions on the school level. At least that was so then.

Finally the books arrived. Enough for each of my students to select a LGBTQ young adult book for a book report. We thought this could be a pilot program and then we could offer these books to the rest of the English department. The set of books sitting in my classroom library caused a bit of a stir among my eleventh-grade English Regents classes. Maybe just surprise. But there was certainly some chatter among the students.

The first day I presented the books to my classes I was concerned. Of course I had heard anti-gay remarks. Not too long before, students disparaged Shakespeare because the painting in the textbook showed him with an earring and long hair. In their eyes, he was clearly gay. (Interesting that today that style is considered cool.) I always gave students my mini-lecture about not judging others, not using pejoratives. My stance then was, since everyone is equal, we do not notice differences. It was the "I don't see color" approach. As I learned later, of course, people of color as well as LGBTQ people want to be recognized for who they are.

On the first day I presented a range of books with gay characters. I wanted students to choose one of them to read for a report. There was nervous giggling, but far less than I expected. I told them it was okay to be uncomfortable. We are not used to talking seriously about gay issues. This was before *Ellen* or *Will and Grace*. But, to my surprise, the students managed to read the books and report on them both orally and in writing. Best of all was that some of the books disappeared from my classroom library. I always thought it was a good sign that students wanted the books enough to "borrow" them.

At first, however, students seemed a bit uncomfortable with the oral report aspect of the required assignment. They shuffled a bit before speaking to the class, however, that disappeared quickly. They related to each of the characters as someone who, like themselves, was trying to make sense of the world and their place in it. I felt as if we had broken some taboo. At least it seemed so in the nineties. Sad to say no other English teacher joined me in this project. The remaining books stayed in my classroom until I left two years later for my self-imposed sabbatical to study for my Ph.D. I gave the books to a colleague, but I don't think they were ever used.

After thirty-some years in the Buffalo Public Schools, some as a substitute but most as a high school teacher, I found my way to Buffalo State College. I was hired in the English education program to teach courses for future teachers. My Ph.D. made this possible, but I did not know that when I began that course of study. It was what I dreamed of, teaching more sophisticated students, having deep, intellectual discussions with colleagues (instead of ones about how awful Susie Q. behaved today). It wasn't that I didn't like teaching in the high school. I loved the students. High school students are fun but at the same time thorny and rebellious. They want to be loved but also push adults away. Yet they are always engaging.

Given the overcrowded classrooms, the lack of textbooks and supplies, teaching in a big city school system was beginning to feel repressive. Also in our district any curricular changes were made from the central administration with little attempt at teacher input. At Buffalo State, by contrast, I could design my own courses. I was even consulted in faculty meetings and asked for advice on shaping the teacher education program. Since I believed being a teacher was a noble endeavor, it thrilled me to contribute to that career in a whole new way. Also, I was excited to share with future teachers my newfound devotion to supporting gay and lesbian students. I was always devoted to supporting African American students, and teaching African American authors, but now I added a new cultural dimension to my teaching.

When I walked into my Introduction to Teaching class on my first day of college teaching, I was astounded. The students quieted down immediately and looked at me expectantly. What a change from high school. I didn't have to wrangle kids into seats, tell them to be quiet and take out their notebooks, move a wise guy who wanted to sit next to his girlfriend back to his assigned seat or ask for missing homework assignments. No bells rang, the classroom phone did not ring, the principal did not make announcements on the PA every two minutes, a clerk did not use it to summon one student out of a thousand to the office. (Wasn't there a phone for that?) Did I say no bells rang? After that class, I sat in my office relishing the quiet. With no Pavlovian bell, I almost missed my next class.

I enjoyed bringing to the college students some of the books and articles I had learned about in my Ph.D. studies, works that analyzed societal pressures arising out of class, color, ethnicity, and gender. I told my students that I strongly believed we teachers had to try to understand all of our students and affirm who they are. We had some lively discussions. Since many of them were the first in their families to attend college, this social analysis was new to them. Sometimes there was debate, which was fine. They were thinking!

One day when I was teaching an Introduction to Teaching Shakespeare class, a male student angrily blew up. In the middle of our discussion of *The Tempest,* he shouted, "I'm sick of hearing about women all the time." He even threw his book on the floor. I was taken aback. Such outbursts usually did not occur in college classrooms. Actually, I had not realized my literary critical lens was feminist. But I realized he was right. That's when I knew I had indeed become such a staunch feminist it seeped into my thinking and teaching without my being aware.

It was a good opening for me. I discussed my kind of criticism with my students and brought in other critical styles for us to examine and discuss. In literary studies, a critical lens slants the way one looks at a text. Despite some conferences, the angry student and I never arrived at an accommodation. He remained angry. And I remained an avowed feminist.

Around that same time, some women students told my (female) office mate and me about a male professor who was stalking and sexually harassing them. We were outraged!

"Let's go to the dean. We will go with you."

They refused, wanting to just get on with their program and away from their harasser. Despite his treatment of women, this professor saw himself as a loyal Catholic. When I wrote a local newspaper op-ed piece about my gay son being discriminated against by the Catholic Church, he harangued me in the department office.

"You know that homosexuality is a sin, a grave sin. You are fine with sin!!" he shouted across the copier I was using, ignoring the secretaries and students around. "What will I tell my grandchildren?" he sputtered, which I thought was a peculiar response.

"Your grandkids will be whoever they are without your advice."

Some years later, this professor's actions caught up with him. He harassed the wrong woman. She complained to the college president. The professor suddenly retired. Too bad it wasn't more public, so that his former students could see he finally suffered a bit of retribution.

Yet he was—and still is—not alone in his attitude toward women and gays. In the Republican Congressional reframing of the health care bill in 2017, the men in the room (there were no women) were willing not only to defund Planned Parenthood but also to cut maternity care as well. Immediately upon taking office, moreover, President Trump rolled back protections for transgender students. It seems to me that negative views toward both women and LGBTQ persons still hold sway, even in the highest strata of our political life

AT BUFFALO State College, since my students planned to become teachers, it became my mission to inform them that they could make a real difference in young lives. I got resources from websites such as GLSEN (then called the Gay, Lesbian and Straight Education Network). Also, I invited representatives from PFLAG and Gay and Lesbian Youth Services (GLYS) to speak to my students. One nice thing about being an instructor on a college campus was that there was little censorship from administrators.

Despite having informed myself about these issues, however, one seminar in 2006 was a huge surprise to me as well as the other education faculty members. During each student-teaching practicum, we brought the students back to campus for a seminar midway through their twelve-week stint. So that all the student teachers, not just the ones I taught, would be sensitive to LGBTQ students, I asked to make a presentation to the whole group. In the sharing portion of the seminar, I was surprised at how many student teachers said they were encountering students who identified as transgender. And this was in 2006! I can't remember the exact numbers. But it was maybe ten or so student teachers out of sixty.

Though I included the T in LGBTQ materials, I had little understanding of transgender students. Speaking at a PFLAG meeting years before, a transgender woman who worked at our local city hall told us about her transition and all the problems she encountered. But I was surprised that student teachers had run into transgender students who were of course going through horrendous social and familial problems. It was clear that we all needed to know more about this population.

Nowadays, I know parents who tell me their children are trans. These parents are struggling to understand and support their children. How very different from years ago when it was not even on our radar as teachers and as parents. As an educator, I believe strongly these issues should be a necessary part of the school curriculum.

At the Emmy Awards in 2016, actor Jeffrey Tambor won an award for his role as a transgender woman in the TV program *Transparent*. In his acceptance speech, he honored the series and all the transgender community for their support. In addition, Caitlyn Jenner has helped bring attention to this minority so often discriminated against. Currently there are many high-profile transgender celebrities, including Janet Mock, Laverne Cox, Chaz Bono, and Jazz Jennings.

In my teaching literature class, I encouraged prospective teachers of English to find literature that reflects the lives of their students, as well as literature that exposes students to the lives of others. The power of literature is so clear to me as a teacher and as a student myself.

I remember a wonderful high school student of mine from when I taught at Hutch Tech. Her family had emigrated from Vietnam under perilous conditions after the war was over, and, finally, found resettlement in Buffalo. She told me she felt so different from her American born friends since she was not allowed to participate in many of the usual high school activities like attending dances, even prom, or going on dates. The conflict of cultures illustrated in the novel *The Joy Luck Club* by Amy Tan really spoke to her.

"This is my life," she said.

Christopher saw his experience reflected in literature for the first time in Edmund White's *A Boy's Own Story*. My students at East High School saw their lives reflected in books by James Baldwin and Richard Wright. As Lucille Clifton and Toni Morrison said, they started to write because they did not see books by people of color like them. At first they did not even realize that most authors were white men. All through my own English degree studies, at both D'Youville and later in the master's program at Buffalo State, I read the Western canon. They wrote great classics of course, and I loved the stories. Oh, yes, I did read the occasional Jane Austen or Charlotte Bronte. But mostly I read the dead white men like Hemingway, Dickens, Tolstoy, and Fitzgerald.

As an older woman, I found it empowering to encounter so many current women writers for the first time. Sad to say, it took me many years to find these writers. And when I did, for the first time during a teachers' workshop in 1988, I was astounded. Like Christopher and my students, I found that poets like Adrienne Rich, Margaret Atwood, Lucille Clifton spoke to me in a vital way. When I met friends who introduced me to women poets from a variety of ethnic backgrounds, I felt as if I had come home. I discovered Sandra Cisneros, Naomi Shihab Nye, Joy Harjo, and Audre Lorde; their experiences of otherness, of crossing boundaries, seemed familiar in some ways to my own experience as a working class daughter of an old-fashioned Italian American family. Sandra Cisneros of Mexican heritage, Naomi Shihab Nye who is part Palestinian, Joy Harjo a Native American and Audre Lorde of African American descent all speak of their otherness, of not being part of the literary canon and of the difficulties of writing in a patriarchal culture. They somehow helped me to see that my small voice could possibly be heard and maybe even read.

A wonderful local teacher and poet, Jimmie Gilliam, held a workshop on writing poetry in 1989. There she introduced me to *Stealing the Language* by Alicia Ostriker. This book became my bible for years. Ostriker, a poet herself, carefully argues and illustrates how women poets in the last half of the twentieth century began to write and share their own experiences.

As poet Muriel Rukeyser said, "What would happen if one woman told the truth about her life? The world would crack open." It was so freeing. Maybe a woman born without a tradition of literature in her home, without the proverbial father's library, could write, too. That is someone like me. Even now, a group of us from that 1989 workshop continue to meet. We struggle each week with this need to tell our stories even if we are "stealing the language" from men and from elites. We grew up not seeing ourselves and, worse, not missing ourselves.

"Mimi, face it. Reading is dead." A teenaged grandchild told me this not long ago.

"Oh, you cut me to the quick!" I replied.

To me literature was the savior of my limited world as a kid. As a teacher, I have been devoted to bringing literature to students. It helps us to see our own world and to appreciate other worlds. Now that we have become a visual culture, maybe movies, television, and the internet will do this. But I am partial to literature.

In 2017, the television miniseries *When We Rise* showed how hard the fight for recognition has been for the LGBTQ community. In the past thirty-plus years, there have been enormous strides. But there is still much work to be done. The battles continue but in different forms. It is still so important for teachers and schools to provide safe spaces for LGBTQ students and to educate all students on human differences. Literature can be critical in doing this.

Since I retired from teaching, I have presented one-hour classes in senior citizen centers in our community. Unlike many of my colleagues, I found retiring difficult. These classes give me a chance to teach again. Consequently, my mission now is to share works that folks might not otherwise read. My favorite presentation is on current memoirs. In it, I can talk about books that tell the experiences of often underrepresented voices. I include Sherman Alexie, a Native American; Roxane Gay, a lesbian of Haitian roots; Sarah Smarsh, a poor farm girl; and Clemantine Wamariya, a Rwandan refugee. All authors that my largely white audience of senior citizens may not know. Shamelessly I also promote this book—the one you are reading—and, in doing so, show photos of our family and talk about our life. Since so many of us live in separate silos of experience today, it seems to me that literature builds the otherwise missing bonds we need in a civil society, the important connections we need with our fellow travelers on the earth.

CHAPTER 16
Christopher: Commitment

Many of the males who have homosexual histories are acutely aware that they are transgressing social custom and engaging in activity which has a certain amount of peril attached to it if it becomes known to the society in which they live. Consequently, many such males become oversensitive to the precise situations under which they accept relationships. All of these handicaps make for discord between homosexual partners, and this lessens the number of opportunities for successful relations.

Long-time relationships between two males are notably few. Long-time relationships in the heterosexual would probably be less frequent than they are, if there were no social custom or legal restraints to enforce continued relationships in marriage. But without such outside pressures to preserve homosexual relations, and with personal and social conflicts continually disturbing them, relationships between two males rarely survive the first disagreements.

— Alfred Kinsey, Wardell B. Pomeroy, and Clyde E. Martin, *Sexual Behavior in the Human Male*

Every relationship you are in will fail, until one doesn't.

—Dan Savage

If you were a gay male living in Seattle in the 1990s, the place to be on a Saturday night was Neighbours, a club on Capitol Hill. Beer was cheap, men stripped off their shirts and showed their gym-toned bodies, and by midnight, everyone was dancing, arms in the air, young and free and alive.

I dated a guy who shared a house with another guy who was an aspiring DJ, and, during the week, he would retreat to the basement to practice mixing songs. During the day, both went off to office jobs, but on Saturday nights, the three of us often ended up at Neighbours, drinking and dancing.

I hated it there.

I hated going to the gym, so I didn't have a body to show off. I hated the way I danced. I hated the way men leered at one another. I hated that I didn't feel comfortable leering back.

My idea of a great Saturday night was going out to dinner with friends, and then going to the movies or a play. One actor I kept seeing on stage was this guy named Patrick Sexton. We met briefly at an audition for a play shortly after I moved to Seattle in 1993. He got the part, and I went on to *In the Beginning* and a few other plays in small fringe theaters. Over the next few years, I saw him in several plays and was always transfixed. I developed a bit of a crush. Patrick had a magnetism and energy on stage that was compelling. I found him devastatingly handsome.

In the fall of 1996, I started working as a teaching artist for the Seattle Repertory Theatre. At a training workshop, I ran into Patrick, who was also a teaching artist that year. He claims I flirted with him that day, which is not likely because I was in a serious relationship with someone else at the time. Luckily, a few months later, when that relationship had ended, a mutual friend happened to invite both of us to a play. Patrick was no less magnetic in person than he was on stage. I loved our discussion about the play when we went out for drinks afterward. He was kind, engaging, and a great listener. And he laughed at my jokes, a big, hearty, throw-his-head-back laugh that made me swoon.

Our first date was on Father's Day in 1997. Neither of us was spending any time with our dads that day. Mine was in Buffalo, probably crying over his grill because neither of his sons was there to celebrate him, and Patrick's father had died of cancer ten years earlier. Our talk, however, did turn to fatherhood.

"I'm the oldest of six kids, plus two steps," Patrick said. "I don't know how my mom managed, because my dad drank a lot and commuted two hours each way to work from Long Island to New Jersey. When I have kids, I don't want more than three."

"You want to be a dad, too? When I came out, my mom made me promise I would have children someday."

This is not usually first-date conversation, especially not for two gay men in 1997. Having children was the furthest thing from the minds of many gay men. Neither of us knew any gay men, single or coupled, who were raising children, but the idea that I had met someone else who wanted children as much as I did was very attractive to me.

Patrick laughed his big laugh at all my jokes and made me laugh so much that I didn't want the afternoon to end. After brunch, we went roller blading along Lake Washington Boulevard, laughing and talking about plays we had recently seen. I was definitely flirting. Once again on a late spring day, promise and possibility floated in the air.

Sure, it was new. Sure, I had only recently split with my ex. But I am pretty sure that I knew from that day that Patrick was the man for me, so it didn't seem one bit strange that, on our second date, we had dinner with his best friend, Gina. Or that I took some photos of him in my apartment that I could show Mom and Dad and my friends when I flew to Buffalo for my brother's wedding that July. Or that Patrick decided to accept my invitation to the wedding and flew out to join the festivities.

Before he arrived, Mom took a break from the planning and preparations to listen as I went on and on. "He's an actor. And he's super smart. And a great listener. We just have such a great connection. Oh, and he's from a big Italian and Irish Catholic family from Long Island."

"I've never heard you talk about someone like this before," she told me over coffee in the kitchen of my childhood home. "He must be pretty special."

"He is, Mom. He is."

At the wedding, I chatted with the lesbian Unitarian minister who told me about some of the commitment ceremonies she had recently officiated. My grandmother took an instant liking to Patrick, teasing him because his family was Sicilian and not properly Italian like hers.

I was my brother's best man, and I proudly recited a poem that Mom wrote for Dad about their own marriage.

*We dance the cha-cha in the dim lights
of my parents' house one day in 1964.
The record blares* Oh baby oh baby
do you wanna dance *and we hold tight,
swirling around their living room
on the rose rug already threadbare
from so many steps so many broken rules
After an embrace it's time to go
and we begin to plan tomorrows
in the hall next to the shuttered milk box
under a square of light from a naked bulb.*

*Then a future twirls in our heads
before sick babies and a dying father,
before one son in Africa,
and one across the continent.
Aches of age grow in rooms we build
and some friends die too soon.
Now the morning sky looks bruised;
a moonlight rim slips through the window.
In our house we fold into each other
every night to dream the cha-cha
As we wait for those next steps;
Do you wanna dance oh baby*

I can see now the confluence of many strands of my life intersecting that day, comingling and spreading out toward new horizons. Our family and friends were there to celebrate the union of Mark and his wife, Barbara. I had chosen Mom's poem that so sweetly reflected my parents' own marriage, from its *oh baby oh baby* beginning to the sick babies and aches of age. When I was young, I spent countless nights sleeping on the floor in my parents' bedroom while they were folded into one another on the bed. It was exactly what I fell asleep dreaming about, my own person to fold into. Mark now had Barbara. Sitting there in the front row, staring back at me, was Patrick. I hugged him tight after the ceremony. That night, we danced under a tent in the humid Buffalo summer. We laughed and toasted. I was thrilled to share my family's milestone with this new—yes, I said it—*love*.

Later that year, when Patrick and I traveled to Long Island for Thanksgiving, I met his family. In many ways, they were the exact opposite of mine. Big and loud, they woke early and got the day moving right away. In my house, the day didn't usually start until late morning, after coffee had been consumed and the newspaper or a book read. Most in my family were Democrats, and many in his were Republicans. My family had always lived in the city while his family made their home in the suburbs. But there was so much about his family that was familiar. There was teasing and plenty of laughter. You showed love by eating Mom's cooking. Nothing came before family.

During our visit, Patrick's sisters were home from college for the long weekend and told stories that had me in tears of laughter. Aunts, uncles and dozens of cousins streamed in and out of the house all weekend. Patrick's mom never left the kitchen and was always prepared to feed lasagna or a roast or a tray of appetizers from Costco to anyone who arrived.

There were some challenges, though. Although Patrick had been out to his family since he was a freshman in college some twelve years before, he had never brought a boyfriend home. I felt a bit like an odd curiosity, on display and sure that I was being judged. I convinced myself that his family was staring at me like some strange object brought back as a souvenir from a trip abroad that seems out of place in the familiarity of home.

House rules, set down by Patrick's mom and her second husband, dictated that no unmarried couples would share a bedroom. The creaky floors, and the fact that Patrick was sharing a bedroom with his teenage brother, prevented any late-night trysts.

I hated not being able to fold into Patrick at the end of the day. But I became fast friends with Patrick's sisters and raved about his mom's food, which was really good, so that was easy. The weekend went by in a blur. I called Mom from the airport and gushed about the visit.

"It's just like our family. I mean they're completely different. But it was so similar."

At Christmas that year, Patrick and I split our time away between Buffalo and Long Island, spending several days prior to Christmas with Patrick's family, still sleeping in separate rooms, and then flying on Christmas Day to Buffalo. In March, we returned to Long Island to attend Patrick's brother's wedding. When we returned to Seattle after dancing at that wedding, we decided to move in together.

In April 1998, I turned thirty. Finally, I found myself trying to figure out what I wanted to do with my life. I didn't have a steady job and was making a living working in a part-time administrative role for the Seattle Children's Theatre while piecing together other teaching and acting jobs. Wanting some sort of career, I eventually decided to go to graduate school to become a teacher.

By Father's Day in 2000, Patrick and I were engaged. Sort of. We were engaged to commit ourselves to each other, not engaged to be married. The idea that same-sex couples should be allowed to marry had not yet become a part of the national consciousness. Massachusetts was the first state to legalize marriage between same-sex couples, but that would not occur for another four years.

The straight world was mostly unaware of all that. Patrick's cousins on Long Island, for example, were astounded when we told them we couldn't get legally married.

"Even in Manhattan?" one asked, incredulous.

Our best friends Doug and Paul had a commitment ceremony in the summer of 2000 that looked and felt just like the weddings of our neighbors, cousins, family friends, and brothers. There was a ceremony, presided over by ministers from the United Church of Christ, and there was food, a toast, and dancing. People got dressed up. There were gifts. Patrick and I were the best men.

Some of our friends thought that making a fuss and having a commitment ceremony was ridiculous. "A commitment ceremony? Why?" one friend asked. "Of course you're going to be together. Everyone knew that from the beginning. Why do you want to make a big deal of it with a ceremony?"

Many gay men believed that copying any of the heteronormative rituals, like monogamy and marriage and kids, was antithetical to being a Good Gay. According to them, being gay is fabulous and transgressive and thankfully different from all that straight bullshit. If you were able to make it to adulthood despite growing up gay in a culture that bullies and demeans and calls you abnormal, why would you buy into the societal institutions that perpetuate discrimination and homophobia?

I understand this perspective. I agree that, in many ways, straight people have made a big, fat mess of marriage and raising children. The hallmarks of contemporary American society after the seemingly perfect 1950s include an inability of members of the opposite sex to communicate effectively, an epidemic of acrimonious divorces, and a whole lot of kids who become unwitting pawns caught between feuding parents. Young couples rush to the altar, but end up feeling isolated and trapped—sometimes within a few years. If there was no societal pressure to tie the knot, why buy into something that many straight couples claimed to want, but, in short order, bailed on?

There were members of my extended family that had marital struggles. We were not immune to alcoholism, unfulfilled dreams, and the wide variety of struggles that lead to ruined marriages and suffering children. Despite all of that, what I saw in my extended family appealed to me. There was so much I appreciated about my whole family, and I couldn't imagine an existence that included not just Mom, Dad, and Mark, but my grandparents, aunts, uncles, and cousins. We laughed a lot. We spent lots of time together and seemed to enjoy one another's company. We had each other's backs. We were by no means perfect, and at times the closeness seemed too close. I sometimes found the roles expected of me confining and limiting, even if I couldn't quite articulate that when I was a kid. But when all was said and done, I wanted a seat at my family's table. And I wanted my spouse sitting next to me.

So how could I reconcile these conflicting perspectives? The modern family was a mess, but I still wanted to be a part of it. Marriage and the family unit needed an overhaul, a fresh perspective. Maybe this is where the gays could be of assistance.

After we had dated and lived together for three years, I was even more certain that Patrick was the one for me, and, after attending Doug and Paul's commitment ceremony, I knew I wanted that for myself. Patrick felt the same. Our answer to the question "Why do you want to have a commitment ceremony?" was "Why not?" If we were going to make a commitment to one another, then we decided that we wanted it to be public. Let's celebrate this, we thought, and not hide.

While we were planning our commitment ceremony, I was in the final stages of my teacher certification program. Shortly before the program ended, a lawyer who worked for the state teachers' union visited one of my courses to share his experience representing teachers in various cases. Most of the advice he gave us went without saying: don't use your work computer for illegal purposes, maintain professional boundaries with students, and be aware of potential conflicts of interest.

My ears perked up when he started to address issues around being out as a LGBTQ teacher. In 1991, Washington's then-governor Booth Gardner signed an executive order banning employment discrimination based on sexual orientation, but that didn't necessarily mean, a decade later, that being an out gay teacher wasn't an issue.

"While you cannot be fired simply because you are gay, during the first few years in a district it is very easy for teachers to be let go," the lawyer told us. "An administrator can find something about your teaching practice that can be used as a reason to end your contract, and it can be very difficult to prove that the real reason for your dismissal is your sexual orientation."

Essentially, his advice was this: *Don't come out and you will have a better chance of staying employed. Later, when you have a permanent contract in a district, then you can think about being out to staff and students. At that point, give me a call if you run into problems with discriminatory behavior.*

This was a sobering thought. I had been out of the closet for more than five years, and in the theatre community there was never a question of being closeted. I could not imagine refraining from talking about Patrick with colleagues or changing his name to Patricia, both of which were offered as possible methods for staying in the closet. I knew that, besides seeming ridiculous and shameful, it would be more than I could manage. I would certainly slip up with pronouns or names at some point.

Hiding from colleagues was only one issue. Part of my desire to become a teacher was to become a visible gay presence in the school community. I had never had a teacher who was openly gay. Wherever I ended up teaching, I wanted gay or questioning students in my classes to have an experience different from mine. Also, how would the hearts and minds of straight students change if they never had experiences with gay people?

By the spring of 2001, I had my certification and was working on my master's project, a study of LGBTQ educators. I wanted to learn directly from others who were already in the profession, not by reading about them in books. I conducted oral history interviews with five openly gay and lesbian educators, charting their challenges and successes in the classrooms and school communities where they worked.

While conducting my interviews, a clear picture of public schools at the end of the twentieth century emerged. Much as they did when I was a student, schools had their fair share of homophobic students and staff. A lesbian I interviewed spoke about derogatory comments directed toward her in her classroom as well as in the teachers' lounge. A gay male teacher mentioned that when a student tagged his portable classroom with the slur "faggot," the maintenance crew didn't paint over the entire word. Instead, they only repainted the letters, so that instead of seeing faggot in black spray paint, it was clearly still there in white paint on a tan-colored background. The message was, on all accounts, clear.

On the whole, however, the experiences of these teachers were positive. They spoke about the various ways in which they had come out, and more often than not, how supportive and welcoming staff, students, and families had been. One teacher I interviewed spoke about the day he inadvertently came out to a class of middle school students. Expecting to come to school the next day to angry emails from parents and a possible visit from the principal, he found the exact opposite. His inbox contained a heartfelt, positive parent email. In the end, it was a non-issue.

In June 2001, I received my Master's degree in education and was offered a teaching position beginning in the fall at The Center

School, a small Seattle public school in the shadow of the Space Needle. As an arts-focused school, we would be partnering with the organizations on campus where I had been working for years. I was elated!

Patrick and I were in the final stages of planning our commitment ceremony that spring and early summer. The planning was similar to what my brother had gone through for his wedding. The same kinds of decisions needed to be made and the same details taken into account. What was our budget? What was the best venue? What would we wear?

We also spent time discussing the political act of using the term *commitment ceremony*. We were not getting married because it wasn't legal at the time, though our big day would look very similar to the many other weddings of straight friends, siblings, and cousins we had attended. Our commitment to one another was going to mean the very same thing that their weddings meant to all of those people. The big difference was that marriage meant a union between two individuals that was legal under the law, and we, as a same-sex couple, were outlaws.

Mom and Dad sympathized, to a point. They would listen patiently, but then try to move on to more pressing questions: Had we found a hotel that could accommodate their friends from Buffalo? What were the plans for the rehearsal dinner? Would there be a full bar or just wine and beer at the reception? Patrick's mom, who had agreed to cater the rehearsal dinner, was more concerned about where in Seattle she could find the appropriate canned tomatoes for her sauce. (Not convinced she would be able to find something she liked, she decided instead to make all the food on Long Island and bring it with her in insulated bags on the airplane to Seattle.)

August 12, 2001, was a stunningly brilliant Seattle day. Family, friends, and colleagues crowded the deck of the *Skansonia*, an old Washington State ferry boat moored on Lake Union in the middle of the city. Patrick's siblings, aunts, and uncles, and his eighty-year-old grandmother watched from the front rows as his mother walked him proudly down the aisle. Mark and Barbara and my aunt and cousin looked on while Mom and Dad escorted me. In matching white linen suits, we held hands under a canopy of deep purple hydrangeas. We listened to blessings from our grandmothers and our good friends. My dear friend Colette read a poem written by Mom that said in part:

> *Watch plants grow beneath your window*
> *in spring luscious with lilacs and lilies*
> *Remember peonies that open and open*
> *large in the rooms you share*
> *expanding to merge your lives*
> *in the homespun joys of everyday*

We made our vows to one another. Said it was forever, good and bad, sickness and health, and all the rest, just like countless others have done before us and will continue to do. Patrick's dear friend Gina sang about how our love was here to stay while we danced our first committed dance. Our moms cut in, and we danced some more. Doug and Paul, returning the favor of our having been their best men, toasted us. It was a great day.

Less than a month later, I started my new job as a teacher of high school English. During the second week of school, terrorists flew planes into the World Trade Center, the Pentagon, and a field in Pennsylvania. The excitement of our ceremony, and the fun of our Hawaiian honeymoon, quickly faded.

All teachers will tell you that the first year is a trial by fire. The certification program, with its short internship, does little to prepare teachers for the daily demands of the classroom. Somehow, with hard work and determination, you learn to make it through.

As if there were not enough going on that year, Patrick and I bought our first home in the fall. We moved, unpacked, and I dove back into work. Sometime in late winter or early spring, I came out to a few students. Word spread quickly. One of the students I came out to proudly reported to me that she told another student that she would kick his ass if he had a problem with the fact that I was gay. It was touching, and it moved me. This young woman's sincerity let me know that she had my back. I had to gently let her know, however, that, while I did appreciate her support, I didn't want her to kick anyone's ass.

What I wanted to do was to start a Gay Straight Alliance (GSA), a club where students could meet on a regular basis to support one another and to discuss issues related to sexual orientation and gender identity. I tentatively approached my principal with the request. While not entirely opposed, she somehow managed to convince me that a better way to go would be to start a diversity club instead. The school was small, and her idea was that the club would be better attended if it welcomed not only LGBTQ students and allies but other minority groups as well.

A grand total of three students attended the first meeting, and none of them identified as LGBTQ. I imagine that students saw right through my lame attempt at being inclusive. I had created a diversity group for everyone, but it ended up serving no one. The group never reconvened.

That spring, I met Lisa, an advocate at the district office who worked with Gay Straight Alliances in other high schools, and she came to our school armed with a letter from the school board indicating that all high schools in the district were encouraged to sponsor one. Twenty minutes later, we were putting the wheels in motion, and within a week we had a GSA that met during lunch hour in the principal's office. Students used a special knock to get in, as early members were concerned that anonymity would help to increase our numbers.

By the end of the year, there was a regular group of five, myself included. Although it was a small and fledgling group, deep down I was thrilled that we were doing this. These five had something that I had never had in high school, and even if it never got any bigger than this, I felt just fine about our little group and what we were doing. It felt transgressive and revolutionary.

Spring comes early to Seattle. As the cherry trees were blooming across the Seattle Center campus, my colleagues and I were hard at work developing engaging curricula for our students. A theater company was producing *The Laramie Project* at a venue across from the school, so we worked with them to study homophobia, discrimination, and hate-crime legislation, all issues that were raised in the play about the 1998 murder of gay college student Matthew Shepard.

Lisa helped me organize a panel of LGBTQ individuals who shared their personal stories of discrimination and bullying. Soon after that, students took up the cause of banning the phrase "That's so gay" from any conversation taking place on school grounds. At the end of the school year, I asked students to write a letter to incoming members of next year's class. One student's letter included the line, "One thing I'll tell you: don't ever use the phrase 'That's so gay.' You will be destroyed." Once again, I could have done without the implied violence, but there was comfort and a sense of pride in knowing that our school community would be one that was diverse and welcoming.

That summer, Patrick and I took advantage of my time off to plant a garden in our backyard. In it was red twig dogwood that bloomed big each summer afterwards, as well as a spot in the sun toward the rear of the yard where I loved to sit in an Adirondack chair and read the Sunday paper.

On August 12, 2002, we celebrated our first anniversary. Two weeks later I went back for my second year as a teacher. On the first day of school, I introduced myself to my class: "Hi! I'm Mr. Drajem! I was born in Buffalo, New York, and moved to Seattle almost ten years ago. This is a photo of me and my partner, Patrick!"

Chapter 17
Linda: Marriage

[Most historians agree that] marriage and family have been in violent flux throughout history, the rules constantly shifting to fit each culture and class, each era and economy.
—E.J. Graff, *What is Marriage For?*

Between the mid-eighteenth and the mid-twentieth century, the social functions and internal dynamics of traditional marriage were transformed. The older system of arranged, patriarchal marriage was replaced by love-based male breadwinner marriage, with its ideal of lifelong monogamy and intimacy.
— Stephanie Coontz, *Marriage, a History: How Love Conquered Marriage*

At age thirteen, when Grandma was married off to Grandpa, she surely did not think it was for love. She barely knew him. He came to the tavern Grandma's parents ran on the rough waterfront of downtown Buffalo, saw Grandma, and told her father he wanted to marry her. Grandma's family was poor and had too many girls, so her parents eagerly married her off to the shoemaker just off the boat from Calabria in Italy. Grandma's three younger sisters had similar fates. The word was Grandma did better than her sisters because her husband did not beat her, but he did leave her with three children, and pregnant with the fourth. Grandma was only twenty years old. The story was that he went back to see his ailing father in Italy. He spent four years there, caught up in World War I. Grandma's family almost starved. My mom said she did not meet her father until she was almost five.

Many years later, I was appalled when my mother's uncle told me that Grandpa did not go back to Italy because his father was ill, as I had been told, but left in a fit of pique at Grandma for some reason. Surely he must have known that his growing family would have difficulty surviving without his support. And they did. My grandmother had to place her three boys in an orphanage for a while because she could not feed them.

My mother proudly described her own marriage to my father as a rebellion against the belief at the time that she had to marry someone her father selected. Against the wishes of her parents, my mother eloped with the love of her life. As a young woman, I carefully considered marriage. I met Bob when I was on the cusp of turning seventeen. We dated for five years, so I felt sure he was right for me when we married. Our marriage has been part of our entire adult lives. It's not too much to say that we grew up together. By the time we were thirty, we had two kids, a house, and a mortgage. It's been almost fifty-five years. Marriage and commitment have been front and center for us. For Christopher, I did not think marriage was possible, but back when Mark was engaged, Christopher sent us this letter:

February 1997

Dear Mom and Dad,

Thanks so much for a wonderful weekend. I was so happy to be part of the festivities [Mark and Barb's engagement party]. Thanks for helping—in a very big way—to make all that possible. You guys are such amazing parents; I count myself very lucky to have such loving and caring role models. When I decide to settle down and share my life with someone, I know that I want that person to be an integral part of my extended family. I want to share that person with you, and want that person to meet all of my friends and family in Buffalo. In short, I want everything that Mark and Barbara have (short of a marriage license).

For some reason, I've never considered having anything less. So, sometime in the future, you'll have to go through all of this planning and parties and ceremony again.

Love, Christopher

At that time, marriage equality was not even on the horizon for same-sex couples. Even commitment ceremonies were rare and brave. (It's amazing how fast things have changed for the better!) When Christopher found Patrick, we were all pleased. They seemed to be in love almost immediately. When he brought him home soon after they started dating, Patrick fit right into our family. He and Christopher seemed so happy. But marriage was not even a thought then.

On August 12, 2001, however, they had a commitment ceremony. Since gay people could not marry in Washington State, nor in any other state at the time, a commitment ceremony was a brave and political act. Christopher and Patrick had their vows solemnized on a sunny summer day aboard a decommissioned ferryboat with the Seattle skyline in the background. It was a joyous celebration of two beloved people joining their lives. But it was more than that, too. It was a public celebration that affirmed them for who they are and shared their commitment to each other with all the people they care about—a huge step in a long journey.

Many longtime friends who watched Christopher grow up made the cross-country trip. We were thrilled that they did. My sister Judy, who never travels, came along with my niece Lillian. Patrick's mom made trays of chicken parmigiana and brought it on the plane in rolling containers. His brothers, nieces, sisters came, as did his aunts and uncles. In this way, the commitment ceremony was a celebration of our growth as well as a family party for beloved sons, nephews, brothers, friends. Most of us had come from solid, working class Catholic roots. But old homophobic prejudices that might have been there because of those beginnings had disappeared. Christopher and Patrick led the way on our own journey of growth.

Although we all called it a commitment ceremony, this was my son's wedding. He thought it would make a statement by pointing out the injustice of gay and lesbian couples' inability to marry legally. In reality, my husband and I got caught up in all the nitty-gritty of planning a wedding. Though we knew that calling it a ceremony instead of a wedding might have political overtones, we were basically worried about whether the food and drink were going to be adequate. To us, it was no different from the planning as we had done for Mark and Barbara's wedding a few years before.

Bob and I walked Christopher down the aisle. Tears filled my eyes. Yes, I thought as I looked out on the sun shining on Lake Union, it is indeed a wedding but much more, too. We ate from a lavish banquet table. There were cupcakes piled high next to a wedding cake with two smiling plastic men on the top. There was a friend's band. The guys had their first dance. Their best men gave moving toasts that brought everyone to tears. Then the mothers got their dance with their sons. Everyone was in such a good mood. That night, back at the inn that we had taken over with all our friends and family, we had another joyous meal. Festivities went on into the next day. It was like the old-fashioned, three-day weddings from our ethnic past. But we also knew in all the celebrating we were committing ourselves to them in a new way. We felt rather than said that our family would have a different shape now.

The future I feared my son would never have, one that includes home and family, fell away that day. I thought he was brave to commit himself to another man when so many societal forces did not honor their love. Little did I dream that fourteen years later the reality of legal marriage could be his. In 2015, the Supreme Court made marriage equality the law of the land.

My background in history and literature tells me that the conception of marriage has changed over time. I know that marriage used to be the granting of protection to women from rape by a variety of other men. From the Middle Ages up until the last century, it has provided protection of property for the preservation of wealth. It has served many other purposes over time, not the least of which is providing for the propagation of children and caring for the elderly.

Arranged marriages and ensuring that the next generation has their property rights are not the norm now. In the West today, the desire for love and companionship is the foundation of marriage, and that was behind the demand for marriage equality for gays and lesbians. When marriage became more about love than producing heirs, then of course gay people should have the right to marry. Now some members of the LGBTQ community feel that marriage is an anachronism, a throwback to the patriarchal preservation of wealth, but such a belief does not negate the civil rights aspect of marriage. Marriage equality for all, including same-sex couples, has been protected by law in many European nations for years, including the Netherlands, Spain, and Belgium, among others.

Surprisingly, the Supreme Court's affirmation of marriage equality has had a measurable effect on suicide rates among children who identify as LGBTQ. An American Medical Association study found that between 1999 and 2015, the rate of suicide attempts by gay high school students declined in states that affirmed same-sex marriage. The lead researcher of the study observed that "laws that have the greatest impact on gay adults may make gay kids feel more hopeful for the future." What an amazing unintended consequence for a fragile youthful minority.

For me as a cradle Catholic, the Church's dismissal of my son and his family has been profoundly hurtful. The previous pope, Benedict, called homosexual unions "gravely disordered." In the beginning of his papacy, the current pope, Francis, seemed so open-hearted and welcoming to all. In his 2016 encyclical titled "The Joy of Love," however, he states that there are "absolutely no grounds" for seriously recognizing "homosexual unions." Here is a pope who seemed to embrace all. Early in his tenure Pope Francis famously said, "Who am I to judge?" in reference to gay priests. I am so disappointed that he closed the door on same-sex unions. I guess I will always be moved and inspired by Jesus' message of love and forgiveness. Maybe I will remain Catholic in some ways. I find it hurtful and infuriating to have my religion used as a weapon to discriminate against my son and so many other gay people.

Not too long after the commitment ceremony, Christopher began to talk about all the thousands of civil rights not afforded to gay couples because they could not legally marry. He made it clear to me that so many federal benefits accrued to married couples, such as inheritance rights, taxes, social security, and over a thousand others. But I was skeptical that these injustices could ever be addressed in our lifetime. On an emotional level, however, and despite all the legal benefits, I did not think it was needed. Christopher and Patrick were already married in the eyes of family, friends, and most especially in their own hearts. And we'd had that lovely ceremony.

During the swirl of debate before the 2015 Obergefell v. Hodges Supreme Court decision, my perception of the issue changed. I was surprised at how much. To have legal support grants a legitimacy that is emotional, psychological, and legal. I know that Christopher's family now has the protections afforded by the state and that is not a small thing. So there are financial benefits as well as the benefit of being seen as equal in the eyes of the state. They are not second-class citizens. When I think of Christopher and Patrick as married now, I realize not only their family and friends know of their commitment but so does everyone they meet.

A sacrament in the Catholic church is an outward sign of an inward change. It feels to me that Christopher and Patrick have indeed participated in the sacrament of marriage. That change is their lifelong commitment to each other. Maybe it appeals to the old ingrained Catholic part of me. When I hear or read about other same-sex couples who are married, I feel the same. There is a sacred permanence to the bond.

Marriage is important. To publicly and legally proclaim your love and commitment is a brave act with profound consequences for not only the family but also society at large. All citizens should have that right. As former President Jimmy Carter affirmed recently, Jesus said not one word about homosexuality in the New Testament. I believe the Catholic Church and any other religion inspired by Jesus should not just affirm gay people but celebrate their love in marriage as well.

Chapter 18
Christopher: Parenting

Jesus had two dads, and he turned out all right.
—Father's Day card

On the afternoon of October 31, 2003, Patrick and I rushed home from work early, hugged one another, and beamed. We had dreamed of this moment for a long time. Finally—in moments! — our lives would change in new and wonderful ways. For the next hour, we anxiously looked out the window and placed last-minute calls to our moms. We triple-checked the stash of diapers and the bassinet. Finally, we heard the car, rushed downstairs, and, while Patrick stretched out his arms, I snapped a photo. With a smile, the social worker delivered Isabella, only twelve weeks old, to us, and boom—we were parents.

I suppose it wasn't that sudden. We had begun exploring the possibility of adoption since shortly after our commitment ceremony. Although I had just started my teaching career and we had just purchased our first home, Patrick was eager to get started.

"If we don't do this now, we're going to be parenting teenagers when we're pushing sixty," he said. "We won't be able to keep up. And we won't be able to dance at their wedding because we'll be walking with canes."

We felt strongly that adoption was the route we wanted to pursue and agreed that working through the foster-care system fit with our values—and our budget. Overseas adoptions can cost tens of thousands of dollars, and we simply did not have that kind of money. Surrogacy was another option, but that could be very expensive as well. We liked the idea that by fostering and then adopting, we could be helping kids who might need a different family situation than the one they were born into. On the other hand, there was a chance that, if we accepted a child, it would only be for a short time, and that ultimately the child would be returned to the birth family. In addition, there would be certain costs incurred in working with an adoption agency to get certified as foster parents and cover the costs of the adoption process. However, it was far less expensive than the other options, and the state would also help to pay ongoing costs like medical benefits for children that they deemed "at risk." In the end, we decided to move forward with the foster-to-adoption process.

The process to get foster parent certification was time consuming, so I agreed with Patrick that we needed to begin as soon as possible. We researched local adoption agencies, attended information sessions, and talked to other interested parents. We settled on an agency called Amara, the only agency in the Seattle area at the time that was willing to work with same-sex couples. We passed their initial interview process, and then the real work began.

For one month, we spent eight hours each Saturday in classes necessary for state foster parent certification. We wrote twenty-page autobiographies for our Amara case worker, answering questions about everything from our childhood experiences to our religious beliefs to how we intended to discipline our children. Our case worker interviewed us, both individually and as a couple. There were additional weekend classes to get certified in first aid and CPR and home visits from the case worker to ensure that our house was suitable and safe for children.

"You know, some straight woman can go out to a bar and get knocked up, and then nine months later there's a kid. Look at what we have to go through to become parents!"

It was my friend Lisa who said this. Around the same time, she and her partner, Jeanne, were also working with Amara to become foster parents. Just to be clear, if you are straight and want to adopt through the foster care system, you are required to go through the same process that you do if you are lesbian or gay, so the comparison isn't necessarily valid. The road to parenting for those in the LGBTQ community holds fewer options than it does for most straight individuals, and any of the available options require deliberate planning and involve lots of jumping through hoops. It was hard not to feel bitter that, as a same-sex couple, we were unable to become parents more easily.

On the day Isabella came into our home, I called my brother to let him and my sister-in-law know that she had arrived. Mark was excited and congratulatory, and recounted how he had told Barbara earlier in the week that we were expecting. He said her reply was "Really? What do they know about parenting?" He told me that he had then asked her, "Well, what the hell did we know?"

Barbara was right to ask. Before all the classes we had taken and all the reading we had done in recent months, I had known nothing about parenting. I had never changed a diaper in my life. I had no idea when a baby transitioned from formula to solid food. I had never considered how I would respond to a daughter who came to me with questions about her period. And on and on.

But, like most parents, I read some books and mostly learned on the job. Patrick taught me how to change a diaper because he had changed his fair share for his sisters. When I was convinced that I would never have a full night's sleep ever again, Patrick and I worked out an alternating schedule of getting up to cover the nightly feedings.

Mom and Dad flew out to Seattle just ten days after we got Isabella to lend a hand. We basked in their immediate and unconditional love for the new love of our lives and delighted in their support for us during an overwhelming time. I struggled to project an air of knowledge and ease, eager to convince them that it all came naturally to me. On the inside, though, I was filled with questions and worry all the time: What was the correct way to hold Isabella so that I wouldn't break her? How would I adequately clean all those parts down there? Is it really all right if she's crying this much? I found it difficult to sleep after late-night feedings and was petrified about intruders or car accidents or strange illnesses that she was bound to contract. Knowing that I had been sick as a child, I had a newfound appreciation for the anxiety and worry that Mom and Dad must have felt. Welcome to parenting: all the power and none of the control.

During my parents' visit, Patrick was on the phone with his mother, and she asked to speak with Mom. It was easy to tell from our end the nature of the questions from Long Island.

"They're doing fine," Mom said. "Yes, everything seems to be going well. They have it all under control. These dads are doing a great job!"

She was either being nice, or we really had her fooled. After years of conversations with other parents, I know that most of us, at one point or another, feel judged. Most parents feel at least some judgment from our own parents, our in-laws, our kids' teachers, their coaches, child care workers, camp counselors, our own friends (whether they are parents themselves or not) and even passersby on the street. But, for us as a male couple, it was easy to feel as if we were being targeted and questioned a bit too excessively.

We are two guys, and for our parents and their parents before them, the role of a father was to get a decent job that would pay well and support the family financially. Women, by contrast, were expected to do the heavy lifting of preparing the meals, cleaning the house, and nurturing the children. It wasn't surprising that Patrick's mother was curious about whether we were up to all the tasks of parenting. From her perspective, I suppose, a family with two dads would be missing out on a critical element: a woman's motherly touch, her warm intuition, an innate desire to foster the lives of her children.

The existence of these kinds of gender stereotypes are pervasive in society and haven't changed a whole lot in the years since we adopted Isabella. For the most part, in families with a mom and a dad, it is the mom who creates the to-do lists, arranges the play dates, and comforts the child with a scraped knee. Usually the men let their wives be the ones to do all that. Certainly more men are cooking these days, or doing more traditionally female tasks like laundry and changing diapers. We knew several straight men who took time off work and let their wives be the ones to work full time, but those men were more often the exception than the rule.

In 2010, while we were in the midst of parenting two young kids—having by that time adopted Jordan, a brother for Isabella—a book came out called *Equally Shared Parenting: Rewriting the Rules for a New Generation of Parents* by Marc and Amy Vachon.

The book points out that for most couples, marriage is either "the traditional marriage with children, in which the man works and the woman stays home, or the 'supermom' marriage, in which the man works and the woman tries to balance a career with the lion's share of the childcare and household tasks." But the Vachons lay out an alternative option, an equally shared one where a couple enters into "[t]he purposeful practice of two parents sharing equally in the domains of child raising, housework, breadwinning, and time for self."

Mom had been the supermom in our family, suffering under the burden of gender expectations that she found personally stifling and that left her feeling inadequate. Since I was young, she worked full time and came home to cook dinner and do laundry. She spent weekends dusting the house, cleaning toilets, and grading papers. Somewhere in there she found time to organize get-togethers for family or friends and maybe, maybe, read a book. I knew it annoyed her to no end when her mother-in-law came over for dinner and commented on her dirty stove, or when her own mother would ask, just as Thanksgiving dinner had ended, what Mom would be cooking at Christmas. I knew because, thank God, she complained to us three men about it when the mothers were gone.

When I was in high school, Mom bought Pierre Franey's *60-Minute Gourmet* cookbook and set out to dazzle us with weeknight gourmet dinners like Chicken Breasts Veronique with Curried Rice or Parsleyed Rack of Lamb with Grilled Tomatoes Provencal. Published by the *New York Times,* the book had a certain literary cachet while appealing to the modern woman who could do it all.

But Mom was wasting her time when it came to impressing her weeknight diners. I bet she regrets the time she spent planning and preparing when she could have been reading Shakespeare or *Pride and Prejudice.* I applauded the effort but liked tacos more than anything and couldn't wait for the nights when she would pull out the frying pan, a pound of ground beef, and the packet of Lawry's taco seasoning. Mark rowed crew in high school and was always raiding the refrigerator. Dad loved meat and potatoes, and I think the curried rice or grilled tomatoes were lost on him.

Mom and Dad had their own version of equally shared parenting, but it took a while for the equal part to be truly equal. When I was young, Dad mowed the lawn, shoveled the snow, planted the vegetable garden, and weeded the flower beds. He washed the cars, paid the bills, and polished his shoes. Odd jobs around the house were his. I seem to remember that my Grandfather—Mom's dad—came over quite often because Dad didn't like ladders. He once shocked himself when he tried to do something electrical before turning off the power at the breaker. Meanwhile, my grandfather could fix just about anything and loved to tease his sons-in-law about their lack of skill in that arena.

Mom, on the other hand, in addition to all those things I already mentioned—cleaning the house, cooking meals, coordinating our social lives—did the grocery shopping, laundry, and ironing. She also, of course, took emotional care of the three guys in the house, while trying to do the same for herself. The thing is, you only have to mow the lawn once a week, whereas laundry and meals and emotions happen daily. I don't know how Mom did it all for as long as she did. It took a toll, and it couldn't last.

As it turns out, men can actually cook and clean and do laundry. There is nothing either biological nor chromosomal, nor is there anything else that prohibits a man from effectively wielding a whisk, dust mop, or iron. So when Mom persuaded Dad to contribute more to the indoor household tasks, she was finally able to give up some of her supermom role. There were a few training sessions on how not to mix lights and darks in the washing machine and some strategizing about all the kinds of tasks you could accomplish while watching a football game, and their roles in parenting became more equal.

I would bet that my dad had a head start of sorts on other men from his generation because his own mother was a bit of a gender nonconformist in her own right. She worked full time outside of the home for many years, and probably had higher lifetime earnings than her husband. She was a force to be reckoned with, and we often joked that she and my grandfather were best known as Mr. and Mrs. Irene Drajem. Dad was the son of a feminist who never called herself that, and he knew the strength and intellect of women from an early age because of the role model he saw in his family. From my perspective, he had always looked at Mom as a true equal. He has nothing but pride in my mother's many career achievements, her poetry, and her Ph.D. in women's studies. He recently told me that he recognizes that Mom did most of the heavy lifting in raising my brother and me.

It never occurred to me that Patrick or I would take up the mantle of supermom. Or superparent. Patrick and I didn't need a book to tell us how to divide up the roles in our house. When we were a youngish, committed couple without kids, we had devised a successful way of managing household tasks. We knew what needed to get done, talked to one another about who was going to be responsible for getting it done, and then did it. The first one across the finish line made the gin and tonics.

Patrick's mother visited our house one year and said that she was so impressed that two men could "keep such an immaculate house." I was both stunned and incredulous. Had she never heard of the stereotype of the gay male, about how meticulous and tidy we are? Had it never occurred to her that her husband could vacuum, do the laundry, or make his own breakfast? Over the years, Patrick and I settled into a pattern that distributed the various tasks of living between us equally. Although spending time together in the kitchen was something that made us very happy, he did the grocery shopping and took on the lion's share of cooking. I scrubbed bathrooms and washed and folded clothes. Together we planted gardens and painted and always ended up collapsed on the couch with a drink in hand.

It's funny that the public perception of rigid gender roles and expectations seems to have shifted only slightly all these years later. Despite having proved that we as a family with two dads could run a household without the benefit of a woman, we were and are still an anomaly. Most of society is still not used to seeing dads out and about without a mom somewhere nearby.

As new dads, we would call up Doug and Paul, who had also adopted a daughter, and head out to engage in the standard activities of families with young kids: the zoo, the aquarium, the science center or children's museum. There we would stroll about with the kids, clutching our coffee and toting a bag filled with diapers and Goldfish crackers and sippy cups of apple juice, happy to be out of the house and in the company of adults.

In the mid to late aughts, it was rare on these outings to spot other families that looked like ours. Even in leftie, liberal Seattle, almost all kids had a single parent or a mom and a dad. If we did spot other gay dads, chances were we knew them through friends of friends or contacts we had made during the adoption process. We knew the community of gay dads in Seattle pretty well, but the straight world around us remained oblivious to our particular family structure. It was not uncommon to encounter a clerk in a shop, a waitress, or even a friendly stranger who would look at us, four middle-aged men and three children, and say, "Oh, today must be Dad's day!" as if we had each brought a kid, and then convinced one of our buddies to tag along for the latest Disney movie.

When Isabella went to kindergarten in 2008, the absence of a mom in our family moved to a new level. Her school was a diverse, alternative public school in diverse, alternative Seattle. But the world of elementary school was still a very sexist place. School was, and probably still is, about moms. Even though there were a few other kids in Isabella's school with two dads, there were none in her grade. Although there were lots of dads who volunteered and drove their kids to and from school, most kids had a mom at home, and it took some getting used to for Isabella's classmates to understand that she didn't.

"Where's your mom in that photo?" one kid asked Isabella in first grade.

"She's got two dads," a friend of Isabella's announced. "Duh."

The year before, in early 2007, we had welcomed our son Jordan to our house, again first as foster parents with the intention to adopt him. He came to us when he was sixteen months old, all smiles and energy, eager to follow the lead of his big sister, and turning our house into an even more cacophonous, chaotic jumble.

When we were close to finalizing the adoption that fall, we had a long meeting at the adoption agency with Bob, his birth father. For a number of reasons, Jordan's mom couldn't parent him, and, uncertain of how he would care for Jordan on his own, Bob had decided to put him up for adoption. In return, the state of Washington promised to do everything they could to place Bob's only child with a family that would allow him to remain in contact with his son. We were that family, and we were eager to maintain a connection with Jordan's birth family. Negotiating just how that would work out was a different matter. We had no experience with this from our first adoption. Isabella's birth family had never been in contact with us, so we entered this meeting with Bob with just a bit of uncertainty and anxiety.

With help from a case worker at the agency, we muddled our way through hypothetical instances of future phone calls and cards and letters. Deciding what seemed comfortable for all of us in terms of visits each year was a tad stickier. We decided to write four yearly visits into the legal agreement and to make a verbal commitment of one every other month. One of the most awkward, and thankfully most lighthearted, moments came when we discussed what Jordan would call his birth dad. Since he already had a daddy (me), a papa (Patrick), and a pops (my dad), we were running thin on choices. Finally, we settled on Papa Bob.

Jordan is supremely lucky to have so many people in his life who love him. He loves his frequent visits with Papa Bob and Bob's dad, whom he calls Grandpa Vic and who is not to be confused with Grandpa, the guy married to Patrick's mother. Isabella and Jordan have an abundance of men in their lives. In addition to the two of us and our families, which include two grandfathers and roughly half a dozen uncles, we have a number of gay male friends (many of them dads as well) with whom we socialize, not to mention the fathers of school friends and neighbors.

I do not believe that this is bad for my children in any way. Kids need love and attention from adults, and they need to have significant role models of loving and nurturing men and women. For Jordan and Isabella, having such a wide variety of supportive adults in their lives can only be counted a blessing. The sheer number of adult males, however, does draw a sharp contrast to the relative lack of adult females. This in no way is meant to disparage the presence of their grandmothers, aunts, friends, and teachers. It merely emphasizes, I believe, the absence of Mom.

Our kids' birth moms exist in our lives like ciphers, ghosts lingering at the edges. They assert their presence and then retreat for a while only to jump out later and rock our world. Jordan lived with both his birth parents for a while, and we have a whole photo album of snapshots of them with a smiling Jordan. Current theories about adoption say that the openness we have with Jordan—the meetings with Bob and Vic, the photos of his birth mom, the stories we tell and retell—will only benefit him in the long run. Day in and day out, however, it is Papa and Daddy who are in our children's lives, and it is a constant concern to try to determine just what information is truthful, age appropriate, and not too much to handle.

Striking this balance is tricky. For Isabella, we communicated the idea that "Mommy couldn't take care of you because she was sick" for a number of years. I always wondered how much sense that made to her. When she was young and just starting school, Isabella would fixate on something like why she wasn't allowed to have candy and treats any time she wanted. How could we expect her six-year-old brain to understand the myriad reasons a mother or father might end up not being in a position to take responsibility for parenting their child? When she was almost nine years old, our pat response started to wear thin. Was Mom just sick? With what? A cold? The flu? Chicken pox? These were ailments she knew about. If she was sick with one of these, then perhaps when she was better, Isabella would be able to go back to her.

When Isabella felt most stressed or anxious, her desire for a connection with her mom seemed to increase. During a particularly challenging time when she was about ten years old, we found a letter in Isabella's room that read "Mom, I love you. Please come and get me. Love, Isabella."

Patrick and I read books about adoption and attended workshops where we heard from experts who described the challenges adopted kids face and what adoptive parents can do to help them feel attached and loved. We found solace and comfort in these resources. However, nothing could prepare us for the experience of watching our baby experience the pain, hurt, and incomprehension up close. The day after we found the note, we hugged and kissed our little girl, who was now getting to that age when she didn't necessarily want her parents to hug and kiss her. Not knowing what else to do, we scheduled an appointment with Miss Kristie, a therapist that we had been seeing with Isabella for a few years. This would be an appointment with just us parents. We needed to know how to navigate this particular challenge, how we might make it better. When your child hurts and is in pain, your number one priority is to ease the pain.

Miss Kristie assured us that it was a wonderful thing, as well as an essential part of the grieving process, for Isabella to be able to express her sadness and feelings of loss. Her sadness and mourning in response to the loss are uniquely hers. I've felt but a fraction of it in my experience, and on some days it is enough to overwhelm me.

As her parent, however, I feel a sudden affinity with the experience that many moms and dads have when they realize they just need to let go. I'm not just talking about the moment when a child who's become a young adult leaves home. Rather it is the many smaller, but perhaps no less significant times in a child's life when you realize that your power to help, to heal, to take care of it all and make everything better is limited.

This push and pull of stepping in or pulling back, of feeling competent and at the same time certain that there is something lacking, is at the heart of the art, not the science, of parenting. From talking to Patrick as well as Doug and Paul and other gay dads, I know that these feelings of inadequacy are common for many of us. From talking to my cousin and sisters-in-law and lesbian friends who are moms, I also know that they feel just as judged and inadequate as we gay dads do. I know that I judge other parents just as much as I feel judged. Perhaps it's just a part of the territory.

There are days when I feel that Patrick and I are superhero dads. We advocate for Jordan and his challenges in school in a way that nobody else can. We persisted in tracking down Isabella's birth mother and reconnecting with her in a way that was full of love and grace and empathy for her and for Isabella. And then there are days when, like my parents before me, and like every other parent who ever parented, I feel that I've just made a royal mess of it all.

At the public wading pool when Jordan was five, I watched as Isabella and Jordan chased Doug and Paul's daughter Charlotte around and around, splashing in the water and yelling with glee. I thought to myself, *Perhaps they shouldn't be going quite so fast, splashing through the water.* Suddenly, the laughter and splashing was pierced with the sound of Jordan's unmistakable wail. I hurried over, mortified, and attempted to soothe the pain. It was only a small brush burn, and I rummaged in my bag desperate for a bandage to cover it.

Through it all, I sensed the glares of the assembled mothers, their own charges still splashing and laughing. Was there hostility behind their sunglasses? Did they assume that I was just another dumb, hands-off kind of dad, willing to sit back and watch as my kids acted crazy and then got hurt? Did they know I was gay? Was there homophobia? Did they think I had no parenting ability? Did they see me as having a bigger responsibility to ensure the safety of all by taming my wild bunch? Or perhaps it wasn't hostility but simply concern. Were they wondering if I perhaps needed help, but wanted to give me the space to deal with it on my own first?

Looking back, it's easy to imagine that these moms might have been thinking any of these things. It's more likely that they were watching with recognition, a shared understanding of what it means to parent. All the power and none of the control. *That poor guy*, they might have thought. *At least it wasn't my kid today.* And then perhaps they went back to reading their book or texting their friend about coming over later for drinks.

In that moment, though, this public interaction took me right to the place of feeling inadequate. Feeling as if I were being judged, for any number of reasons. Feeling that I just wanted to get out of there, which is what I did.

"C'mon, everyone. It's time to go!"

I shoved things into bags, rolled up blankets, swathed kids in towels, and loaded everything and everyone into the car. Jordan screamed in the car all the way to Doug and Paul's house while Charlotte asked over and over, "Why is Jordan crying?" He didn't stop until we got home. I cleaned out the wound, covered it with a Thomas the Tank Engine Band-Aid, and fed him a popsicle. Isabella said something funny, and Jordan smiled. She said it again, and he laughed. And then he laughed some more.

The three of us went into the living room, sat on the couch, and, with one kid on either side of me, I read to them—for the hundredth time—the story of Tango, the true story of a penguin at the Central Park Zoo that was adopted by two penguin dads.

Chapter 19
Linda: Grandparenting from a Distance

*You only have to let the soft animal of your body
love what it loves.*
—Mary Oliver, *"Wild Geese"*

Thank goodness! I was so wrong when I thought Christopher would not be able to become a dad! He and Patrick actually wanted to be parents right from the beginning of their relationship, which still amazes me. They chose the foster-to-adopt route in 2003. For a few years already, they had been on a list at a gay-friendly adoption agency in Seattle. Religious adoption agencies discriminated against the LGBTQ community and so did foreign agencies. That is sadly still true today. In August 2018, our Buffalo Catholic Diocese declared that the agency that had sponsored adoption and fostering would drop the program because one gay family asked to be considered as parents. One couple! Because New York State law prevents them from discriminating, they would drop the program and shuffle off the children to other agencies. To say that Bob and I were beyond outrage is an understatement. We fired off letters to the local newspaper as well as to the Board of Trustees of that Catholic agency.

Though fostering and adoption laws vary among states, some of them allow religious groups to discriminate against same-sex prospective parents. Since the 2016 presidential election, the list of such states has grown. Georgia has passed such a bill. Kansas and Oklahoma passed bills in 2018. Several other states were considering similar laws in 2019 to allow this kind of discrimination.

There are all kinds of marriages. The traditional model of two parents and a boatload of kids is indeed not the norm any more. In my long career in education, I have seen families headed by single parents, adoptive parents as well as other kinds of arrangements. It might be pretty to think that all marriages include wanted children, that all pregnant mothers care for their bodies and their unborn children, that all biological dads are present to care for their children. But that is not the case. Thankfully, there are couples who are willing and able to adopt children from parents unable to provide the nurturing they need. Thank God there are couples like Christopher and Patrick. There are so many children in the foster care system whose birth parents can't care for them. To have two loving parents eager to step in should be celebrated.

When I got the call in 2003 from Christopher that indeed they had a darling baby girl, I was beside myself with joy. Only a year earlier, Mark and Barbara had a girl, Zoe. Now Isabella was joining our family. For years, grandparents had told me how great it was to have grandkids. Of course I believed them. However, the happiness I felt went beyond the norm. Perhaps that is what every grandparent thinks. In addition, I was secretly happy that now I had two granddaughters. As a mother of boys, I had never been able to buy frilly dresses in pink and otherwise fuss over girls. Yes, a stereotype, I know, but I thought it would be fun to have girls in the family. And it is! Isabella and Zoe are such a joy! The boys, Noah and Jordan, are too of course; grandparents do not show favorites!

Serendipitously, shortly after three-month-old Isabella arrived in their home we were on our way to visit Christopher and Patrick. I was happy to do the baby stuff, change diapers, watch her sleep, walk around with her when she didn't, and rock her in my grandmother's rocking chair, which we had sent to Seattle a few years before. Bob and I were delighted with our baby time.

Seven months later, in June of 2004, we rented an apartment in Seattle, stayed for six weeks, and took care of Isabella each day. We took her on long walks in Seattle's beautiful Queen Anne neighborhood. We planned picnics in the park. We even took this nine-month-old on a boat trip on Lake Union and pointed out the sights to her. Needless to say, she just looked and babbled. She was such a star. Many folks we saw on our adventures stopped to coo over her and to marvel at her beauty. Naturally we agreed.

Sadly, we could not stay. Our life is here in Buffalo. Since then we have crisscrossed the continent many, many times to see Isabella, and a few years later, Jordan. Our staying with them, on the other hand, is an intrusion into their lives. Patrick is always very gracious about sharing his home with us. Christopher, too, of course, but since we are his parents it might make it easier for him. Lucky for us Christopher and Patrick have brought their family to visit Buffalo many times as well.

While my mother was alive, I was conflicted with concern for her on the one hand and my desire to be with our grandchildren on the other. She was in a nursing home because her health was declining, and I felt responsible to at least supervise the care she was receiving. I often felt torn but did not want to miss out on the early years of my grandchildren's lives. Although I still worried about her, Mom encouraged me to go be with my grandchildren.

So I did get a chance to see some important stages of their lives. When she was tiny, Isabella loved to take walks and look for what she called "potato bugs." She meant those beetle-like bugs called pillbugs that curl up at a touch. She loved playgrounds, especially going down the slide with me. Often in the early morning, she would crawl into bed with us. I loved snuggling with her, her curly hair, her unique nutty scents of shampoo, soap, and toothpaste. One time when she was about seven or eight, we wrote notes to each other under the covers in the tea-colored morning light.

Jordan was about eighteen months old when he joined the family in 2007. We went out for a visit shortly after. Isabella gave us a big hug and only then did Jordan toddle over to do the same. As he grew older, he became a Thomas the Train fanatic. As soon as we arrived, he would pull me into his playroom, which the guys had set up with his Thomas trains. Bob and I watched more Thomas videos than we can count. Because they were such important steps in forming their family, of course we had to fly out to Seattle to be present at each child's formal adoption that was followed by festivities.

Christopher and Patrick were great about including us on

weekends and during vacations. Sometimes they would sneak off to a well-deserved night out or even a weekend away. We read books to the children, played board games with them, and took them to the newest Disney movies. Now, even as teenagers, they take turns spending a week with us each summer. These are great times. Bob and I fuss over them, buy them sugary, fruit-flavored cereals that their parents would never allow and take them on adventures each day. And we get to just be with them.

My parents were wonderful role models as grandparents. They just loved my sons and my sister's daughter. Always eager to babysit, they engaged with them on their level. I remember coming home from substitute teaching and finding my mom's living room cluttered with blanket tents she had created for my three- and four-year-olds. The three of them were immersed in a game of make believe. When our grandkids came along, I wanted to emulate my parents. I started curtailing my work at Buffalo State College and then finally resigned. I wanted to be available to be with all four grandkids, two on each coast.

Mark and Barbara have included us as well. Because Barb had to travel for work, we got to take care of Zoe and Noah when they were younger. Sometimes we spent a week or more at their home in Silver Spring, Maryland. We marched in the Halloween Parade when they were little. They live near Sligo Creek Park, so we went there to take walks and to push the kids on swings and watch them go down slides. I even chaperoned one of Noah's field trips to the Smithsonian Science Center, which was fun for me. I made lunches and we both did after-school pickups with other parents and grandparents. It's a joy getting to watch them grow. Now they are teenagers. They still visit us for a time each summer, which is a delight for us. And, yes, we still buy them sugared cereals and anything else they would like!

Mark's and Christopher's families have also taken joint vacations with us. All ten of us together. In the summer of 2018, we gathered at the beach in South Carolina. How wonderful to see Isabella and Zoe share a bedroom, rock together in the hammock, tease each other. Noah at fourteen helped twelve-year-old Jordan with the thousand-piece puzzle Bob started as a family project. Since our sons' families are bicoastal, those gatherings are rare but special. We have reframed our family to extend across a continent and, even more importantly, across the traditional model of heterosexual norms.

Of course we have missed out on some important experiences in our grandchildren's young lives: the first day of kindergarten, class plays, band and dance performances, lacrosse games, and ultimate Frisbee. We've also missed covering for sick days and all those other daily or weekly assignments grandparents who live close to their children take for granted. If I had to choose, I would of course want the daily joy of seeing my grandkids (and their parents). Distance is not easy. My boys got to go around the block to see their doting grandparents. We have to go thousands of miles. But it's a small price to pay for all we have to be grateful for, including the brave men and women who have paved the way, some with tattoos and piercings, some with leather or in drag, and some with their honest words.

Gay men do parent. They do stay connected to their faraway families. And they do a damn good job of it.

Chapter 20
Christopher: Seismic Shifts

No union is more profound than marriage, for it embodies the highest ideals of love, fidelity, devotion, sacrifice, and family. In forming a marital union, two people become something greater than once they were. As some of the petitioners in these cases demonstrate, marriage embodies a love that may endure even past death. It would misunderstand these men and women to say they disrespect the idea of marriage. Their plea is that they do respect it, respect it so deeply that they seek to find its fulfillment for themselves. Their hope is not to be condemned to live in loneliness, excluded from one of civilization's oldest institutions. They ask for equal dignity in the eyes of the law. The Constitution grants them that right.

— Justice Anthony Kennedy,
James Obergefell, et al., Petitioners v. Richard Hodges, Director, Ohio Department of Health, et al. June 2015

As a union of individual state governments, the federal government of the United States has certain powers while others are left to those individual states. Only the federal government can declare war. Individual states retain control over police power. Another power left to the states is the granting of marriage licenses. State constitutions indicate who can marry, at what age, and according to what specific requirements.

In 1990, saying that the law violated the state constitution, three same-sex couples challenged the Hawaiian state law that banned them from marrying. As their case wound its way through state courts over the next decade, other states and the federal government took notice. In 1996, worried about the implications of a favorable outcome in Hawaii for same-sex couples, members of Congress passed the Defense of Marriage Act, known as DOMA. Approved by presidential veto-proof majorities in both the House and Senate, the bill was signed into law by President Bill Clinton.

Section two of DOMA said that no state was forced to recognize the marriage of same-sex couples in other states, and section three declared simply that, in terms of federal law, "the word 'marriage' means only a legal union between one man and one woman as husband and wife, and the word 'spouse' refers only to a person of the opposite sex who is a husband or a wife."

A report by the General Accounting Office published in January 1997 identified "1,049 federal laws classified to the United States Code in which marital status is a factor." When Patrick and I knew that we wanted to be with one another for life, we took it for granted that none of those rights would be granted to us in our lifetime. That didn't stop us from planning our commitment ceremony, which we approached with a devotion that would have put many brides to shame.

Intent on finding helpful resources about a year before our August 2001 ceremony, I went to a local bookstore and looked for the wedding section. There was book after book on every detail and shape and size of wedding imaginable, but there was not one about ceremonies for same-sex couples. I went to the gay and lesbian section, and there, after an exhaustive search, I found it: the *single book* that offered advice for us. I bought it immediately and read half of the book in my car in the parking lot.

Although we didn't get married in a legal sense on August 12, 2001, that is what we consider our wedding day. That is when we celebrate our anniversary. That is the one in the photo album that we show our kids, and the one we reminisce about with our relatives, friends, and one another.

Two years and two months after our wedding, in the fall of 2003, Isabella came into our lives. The following year, when we were sleep-deprived and knee-deep in diapers and baby food, Massachusetts became the first state to recognize legal marriage rights for same-sex couples. It was also the year that there were calls at the federal level for a constitutional amendment that would limit the definition of marriage to heterosexual couples. President George W. Bush, fearful that DOMA would not stand up to court challenges, lent his support to the effort and declared that, "After more than two centuries of American jurisprudence and millennia of human experience, a few judges and local authorities are presuming to change the most fundamental institution of civilization. Their actions have created confusion on an issue that requires clarity."

In early 2007, Jordan joined our family, and that summer our state legislature passed a domestic partnership law, conferring eleven of Washington State's rights of marriage to same-sex couples. When straight people marry, there's a whole host of pretty cool—and practical—benefits that come with the marriage certificate. Most couples don't really think about these when they're registering for china or getting hammered at their bachelorette party. With the 2007 domestic partnership law, card-carrying domestic partners were granted some of these benefits, including the right to visit a sick partner in the hospital, the ability to make healthcare decisions for that partner, and, in the event of the partner's death, the ability to make decisions about the funeral and burial, and the right to inherit the partner's assets.

There were still many other rights that were not included in this first domestic partnership law in Washington State. Individuals were still not allowed to use sick leave to care for a domestic partner and were still not entitled to an injured partner's wages and benefits, much less unpaid wages upon a partner's death. Certain insurance rights were also restricted, including rights under group policies for state employees. This last issue impacted us directly when I took a leave from work to stay home and care for Jordan in 2007. Patrick, a state employee at the University of Washington, was forced to pay taxes on the amount of money that the state was paying for adding me to his health insurance, something that wouldn't have happened if we were straight and married.

Around this time, many committed same-sex couples were sharing stories about traveling to different states in order to get married. In 2004, in addition to the Commonwealth of Massachusetts, a handful of municipalities from New Mexico to New Jersey issued marriage licenses to same-sex couples. When same-sex marriage was briefly legal in Oregon's Multnomah County, one couple we know drove with friends to Portland to tie the knot. A few months later, however, the county revoked their marriage certificate when an Oregon state law was passed making marriage between same-sex couples illegal. British Columbia had legalized marriage between same-sex couples in July 2003, and another couple we know drove for three hours from Seattle to Vancouver, BC, that summer to get legally married after their commitment ceremony—their wedding—in Seattle.

In October 2008, Patrick and I went on our own chase. We slipped away to the Bay Area and got legally married in the Alameda courthouse during that short window of time (June through November of 2008) when California was dabbling in the same-sex marriage business. It was nice to have a break from our kids, nice to visit wine country in early fall, nice to be just a couple again.

We did have strong reasons for wanting to secure the marriage rights conferred by California. New York State had agreed at that point to recognize the marriages of same-sex couples from other states, and, as frequent travelers to visit family and friends in New York, we thought that having some legal standing might be beneficial. What if one of us ended up sick and in the hospital while we were on the East Coast? What if our kids ended up there and we needed to make decisions about their care together? What if… who knows? It seemed worthwhile to gain as many legal protections as we could.

Isabella, who was five years old at the time, was mystified. "I thought you already were married?" she said. Well, yes, sweetie, in our hearts and the eyes of our friends and family, but not legally, not according to the state. "What's a state?" she asked.

When we returned from our trip, my family wanted to know why we weren't calling one another husband. Proposition 8, a statewide ballot proposition in California, passed a mere month after our trip. Marriages between couples like us abruptly ended when the state constitution was amended to include the line that "only marriage between a man and a woman is valid or recognized in California." For many months, it was unclear if our California marriage license meant anything, or if it was null and void as of November 5, the day after the vote. In May 2009, the state declared that Proposition 8 was constitutional, but allowed all same-sex couples who had been married in the few months when it was legal to retain their marriage rights.

Even though we were officially California husbands, I still called Patrick my partner. The legal recognition was nice, but it was difficult for me to call Patrick my husband on a day-to-day basis when Washington State forbade it. It felt awkward and somehow false. *Husband according to whom?* I imagined people wondering. As I saw it, if my home state was not conferring the rights, it was going to be difficult to use the h-word.

New York State beat Washington to the marriage equality punch; legal weddings started there in the summer of 2011. Friends of ours were married on the first day, and, scrolling through their photos on Facebook, I took in the excitement and triumph. Our commitment ceremony and their wedding couldn't have been more different. They brought along only one friend to the courthouse to act as a witness and needed to find someone else in line who would agree to be a second witness. There was no band, no cake, and no pile of presents. The only gifts they received were the legal rights and assurances of a whole state. I sure wish we could have opened that one on our big day in 2001.

As it frequently does in our house, news of our temporary victory in Washington came via the local NPR station in February 2012. I was doing my best to get dinner on the table, with one ear glued to the big report of the day. That afternoon, the Washington State senate had voted to allow same-sex couples the right to marry. I listened as if in a trance as one state senator after the other, both Republican and Democrat alike, spoke passionately about their desire for everyone to have the same chance for love, companionship, and security. I was thrilled, elated, relieved—and proud. I wiped a few tears from my eyes as Isabella wandered in from the other room. "What's wrong, Daddy?" Nothing, honey. Nothing at all.

When our governor signed the bill into law that February, a friend wrote to offer her congratulations. "Will you and Patrick have to make decisions about all the floof, or just elope?" she wanted to know. We already had floof, I explained. We'd had our gay wedding. And, yet... Patrick and I did discuss how we might celebrate this brand-new victory. A marriage certificate with both our names on it, stamped by the state of Washington, bestowing approval and equivalence, would be something to hold precious and dear for a lifetime. It would be something to celebrate.

Marriage confers those numerous rights and benefits that many straight people take for granted, like the ability to file joint federal income tax returns, and the option for spouses to receive social security, Medicare, public assistance, and disability benefits. But the term married gives more than legal rights and benefits. It bestows status and privilege as well. It is a term that communicates a rich and evolving cultural history. It's shorthand signifying all that is unique and mysterious for every couple that is able to claim it. Any adult human being who loves another adult human being should be allowed to be a part of this club, if they choose.

Many in Washington, however, were reluctant to see that happen. Intent on rolling back the law, opponents quickly mobilized. They eventually gathered enough signatures to put Referendum 74 on the November ballot. State voters would have the final say.

News of our permanent victory came on election night in 2012. Shortly after President Obama was reelected, the local news stations turned their attention to our state's legal marriage question. According to the early reports, results were close but favorable for the supporters of marriage rights for all. Although the final count wouldn't be announced until days later, we went to sleep that night confident that our state was part of a historic moment. Voters in Washington State joined those in Maine and Maryland in support of same-sex marriage rights, and all three states became the first in the nation to have voter-approved marriage rights for same-sex couples.

Patrick and I could have decided to do nothing at all about the granting of marriage rights, which would have been just fine.

Under the provisions of the law, same-sex couples registered as domestic partners would have those partnerships automatically converted to marriage after a certain amount of time.

Our good friends Lisa and Jeanne, a lesbian couple with two children the same age as ours, wanted to host a community gathering to celebrate the passage of Referendum 74. When they asked us to join them in cohosting the event, we had some reservations. We were worried that some of our friends might be confused. "Didn't you already get married? Or did you not consider yourself married until now?" When we invited people, we wanted it to be clear that this was indeed a celebration for everyone. We wanted to make it clear at the event that our whole community was stronger because of this leap we had collectively taken.

We decided in the end to join in and celebrate. Ultimately, the party hit just the right note. A community center donated space, and we asked folks to bring food to share and to pay for their own drinks. Some folks dressed to the nines, and others were in jeans and fleece. There were families with kids in tow, couples gay and straight, friends we had known for years, and strangers who wandered in off the street when they saw the signs and rainbow balloons outside. In a quiet room upstairs, you could book a time slot and hold a wedding ceremony, a legal one, with one of several officiants who were on hand. Every time a couple was married, a gong sounded. Patrick and I chose to reaffirm our vows in the company of our kids, a few friends, and Patrick's sister. She signed the legal paperwork as our witness, and we were done. Later, there was a toast, cake, and dancing with our kids.

The toast, written by Patrick and me, went something like this:

> *Some of us gathered here dreamt for a long time of finding that special someone, falling in love, facing our doubt, and then making a commitment.*
>
> *We couldn't wait, and yet we did, never imagining this day, this celebration of marriage equality, would happen in our lifetime. In the meantime, we created our own rituals, celebrated our commitments, and wedded our hearts to our beloved.*
>
> *Today we celebrate that our forward-thinking state of Washington finally recognizes, for the first time, that no individual should be denied the basic right of marriage just because of who they love.*
>
> *This victory is for the LGBT community, certainly, but we recognize that our whole community is stronger because of this leap we have collectively taken. We have, all of us, built a state where we are closer to living in fairness and equality.*
>
> *Words are important. Marriage does matter. Thanks to referendum 74 we leave our children, grandchildren, and generations to come a lasting legacy: the ability to live your wildest dream, love who you love, and perhaps, someday make a vow.*
>
> *Let us all raise our glasses in a toast:*
> *TO LOVE'S TRIUMPH!*

So Patrick and I had a wedding. Another one. It was the community celebration we wanted. A chance to recognize the importance of the term *marriage* and cheer with all our friends who were happy for us, happy for our community, thrilled to live in a historic state at a historic time. We had voted, and love had won.

In June 2013, there was more good news, this time from the Supreme Court. In 2010, a district court had overturned Proposition 8 in California, but it had stayed in effect while appeals wound their way to the Supreme Court. In a sweeping ruling, the highest court in the land upheld the ruling that overturned Prop 8, and same-sex couples were once again allowed to marry in the Golden State. The court also declared Section 3 of the Defense of Marriage Act unconstitutional under the Due Process Clause of the Fifth Amendment. States could no longer refuse to recognize same-sex couples who were legally married in other states, but it would take two more years before the term gay marriage was finally—hopefully?—put to rest, and marriage became marriage, love was love, the end.

On June 26, 2015, the United States Supreme Court handed down its landmark decisions in the case of James Obergefell, who, along with several other plaintiffs, argued that state statutes banning the marriage of same-sex couples in Ohio, Michigan, Kentucky, and Tennessee violated the Equal Protection Clause and Due Process Clause of the Fourteenth Amendment to the Constitution.

In a five-to-four decision, the Court agreed with the plaintiffs, and just like that, marriages between same-sex couples in all fifty states became legal. In his statement to the media after the decision was handed down, James Obergefell said, "It's my hope that the term 'gay marriage' will become a thing of the past, and from this day forward it will simply be 'marriage.'"

Soon after the news of the decision was handed down, I received a text from my friend David: "This is a great day to be an American. Haven't felt that way too often!" A bit later my colleague Kim wrote to say, "I clearly remember telling my GSA students that I wouldn't see this day in my lifetime, but I had faith that they would see it. So happy I was wrong."

I couldn't agree more. I, too, had never imagined Patrick and I would be able to legally marry in our lifetime. Growing up, it was my dream to get married, have kids, and grow old with the love of my life. Then, in coming to terms with my sexuality, I thought my dream was gone.

It was another quotation I heard on that June day that resonated the most with me. The kids and I were visiting Buffalo. Mom and I were listening to the coverage in my parents' living room while Jordan and Isabella occupied themselves with screens and Legos. President Obama spoke from the Rose Garden, celebrating along with us. The last section of his remarks struck a chord.

Obama said that the ruling was the "consequence of the countless small acts of courage of millions of people across decades who stood up, who came out, who talked to parents — parents who loved their children no matter what. Folks who were willing to endure bullying and taunts, and stayed strong, and came to believe in themselves and who they were, and slowly made an entire country realize that love is love."

We—Mom, Dad, Patrick, Mark, Lillian, Aunt Judy, and I—all contributed to that moment. I had enough faith in my family to share who I really was, knowing that they would love me no matter what. I also had enough faith in my colleagues and students to come out at work. All the members of my family embraced me, my spouse, and my children. Each of them has challenged colleagues, friends, and other family members to see the love that Patrick and I share is no different just because we are gay.

As a family, we uncovered the power of truth, integrity, and love, and in a small way contributed to a seismic shift in the history of our nation. Our shift was just a slight tremor, but, in our own small way, we showed those in our world that love is love.

That is something that fills me with pride.

Conclusion—Linda

*When you were small we danced
we sang, wove Zinnias into garlands
played house with tiny plastic people
who never fought and had perfect families.
We created villages of Legos
full of symmetry and peace.
You slept on the floor of our room
when thunderstorms split your rest.
I tried to soothe away all fears
till life pressed in too much for us both.
Did the cocoon I tried to spin
hold you back from saying
your reality?
Now your bravery takes me away,
pushes me into my own flight:
May we both become who we are.*

"Son-dance Prayer"
—Linda Drajem

Back in the seventies a mantra of the women's movement was "the personal is political." Societal structures and beliefs can empower or can be destructive. For me the 2016 presidential election was a devastating example of the later sort. The worst prepared candidate in history beat one of the best prepared, perhaps partly because of her gender. A recent *New York Times* article wondered at great length whether a woman could ever be elected president, despite the many women now running for the 2020 Democratic candidacy.

Hillary Rodham Clinton paved the way for this debate. I first learned about her when presidential candidate Bill Clinton ran in 1992, and Hillary said she didn't want to just bake cookies! How refreshing to see a possible First Lady who was an accomplished lawyer and an advocate for children and families. No beaming Nancy Reagan applauding from the sidelines looking adoringly at Ronnie. Nor a sharp-tongued Barbara Bush who focused on home and family, trotted out now and then for diplomatic occasions. Here was someone who actually had a career!

Oh yes, she suffered great criticism for it, and she did end up baking cookies, but she accomplished so much more. She survived media criticism for everything from her hairdo to her investments, and even Bill's infidelity. She went on to be a senator, a Secretary of State, and actually beat her opponent in the presidential race by three million votes. But she failed to reach the pinnacle of power.

It was and is so disturbing that this woman who I most admire was done in by someone who, besides having no governmental experience, called people names, made unfounded claims, and was openly racist. None of these behaviors have changed these many years into his presidency. In addition, he actually boasted about abusing women and has been accused of rape by several. So while the societal shifts of the past century opened the door to Hillary and to many women, the old forces of sexism remain.

For Christopher the great societal shift of Stonewall opened the doors for him and others in the LGBTQ community. Great strides have been made, like marriage equality, inclusive policies for the armed forces, greater representation in the media, and even celebrities being open about their sexual orientation. Back when Christopher came out, in the wake of AIDS-related panic, it was unthinkable that all of this would happen. Perhaps the biggest surprise of all in 2019 is that an openly gay man, Mayor Pete Buttigieg of South Bend, Indiana, is now running a very credible campaign for president. He is even in the top tier of candidates for the Democratic nomination. None of this would we have imagined back on the that cold March day in 1994 when my beloved son told me he is gay.

But the forces of regression are still there. Though the Supreme Court affirmed marriage equality in 2015, many states now have in place laws that allow discrimination by the ruse of religious freedom. One of the first acts of the current administration was to undo protections for LGBTQ students in place during the Obama administration. President Trump has overruled his own military and ruled that trans persons cannot serve. The person he selected as his vice president has a record of anti-LGBTQ policies as a former governor of Indiana.

For Christopher and me the doors were opened, but now our concern is that they stay open for our children and for others. Both Christopher and I were affected by major societal shifts. And we contributed to them. We did not stay in our insular Buffalo upbringing but branched out in many ways. Moving away geographically and emotionally, to new frontiers.

In 2017, Christopher and Patrick invited us to join their family for part of their month-long road trip from Seattle to California. We joined them and their children in San Francisco. We followed them in our rented car up the coast of California to towns like Windsor and Eureka.

Along the way we went to wineries, beaches, pools and had many lovely dinners at restaurants or in our rented condos. We were delighted to be included in this family vacation. At one stop, Christopher said to all of us, "I have been looking for families like ours during our trip these past weeks."

"Face it, Daddy, there are not many families like ours!" said almost fourteen-year-old Isabella with a big smile.

Yes, perhaps there are not many families like theirs. Gay dads and two kids. But there are far more today than there were back when Christopher came out to his family and his friends. As I have stated, I thought family life would not be for him. Many gay men and lesbian women still believe that. Their choices have been different. But for Christopher, family was the life he wanted. I admire the choices he has made, deviating from the norm for gay men, in that that he has chosen family life. He has chosen a husband who shares his goals. I admire him as a father. I always knew he would be a great dad, but he has gone above and beyond in his efforts to parent children who come from backgrounds that have given them precarious life beginnings.

I value that Christopher supported me on my late-in-life quest to write and to gain a Ph.D., and to teach on the college level. My efforts would have failed without his support, as well as that of

Mark and Bob. My family was invaluable in that rather quixotic quest, especially for a woman of my age.

I especially appreciate that when he came out as gay, Christopher was willing to talk and to listen. He shared no anger or blame, which most certainly could have been the case. He answered questions and continued the conversation. The lines of communication stayed open and helped Bob and me to grow into better versions of ourselves.

Maybe that is the final message of our journey: keep talking and listening, no matter the challenges, of which there are many.

Societal forces need to be expanded so that all of us have opportunities to grow. So, indeed, the personal is political. In this time of great divisiveness, we have to work toward greater change, greater freedom, and not sink into the tribal lines that have hurt so many in the past and still do today.

Conclusion—Christopher

In September 2017, a student of mine at Newport High School tentatively approached me after the first day of class. As all the other students hurried out of the room, he quietly told me that the traditionally female name listed on the roster didn't reflect who he was as an individual and asked if I would kindly use a different name and masculine pronouns when referring to him. I was not only happy to make the change but eager to take it one step further. I contacted the school counselor and asked if there was any way to indicate these changes in the computer system teachers use to take attendance, create seating charts, and record grades. It was simple, the counselor said. All the student had to do was stop by the counselor's office, let them know what name was preferred, and they could make the change right away.

The ease with which this problem was solved astonished me and delighted the student. There was no proof required and no lengthy paperwork to complete. Not even the student's parents needed to be involved. How enlightened. Thoughtful even. I imagined how terrible it must have been for the student on the first day of class, needing to stop and discuss this issue with each teacher. I imagined the frustration of the student when a substitute teacher in the classroom was unaware of the student's preference, or when a school nurse or administrator looked confused. I marveled at the changes in our schools in the years since I was a high school student. How amazing for this student and other LGBTQ students to be alive today.

Of course, that tells only part of the story. The student went on to have a less-than-stellar academic career. There were less-than-supportive family members and teachers to be dealt with as well as inappropriate, probing questions from fellow classmates. He failed the first semester of my class, in large part due to attendance issues. He withdrew from the class at the start of second semester and had to get credit for the course online. He did graduate, but just barely.

He's in community college now. I hope things go well for him there; it seems to be an environment in which a smart, passionate, well-read kid like him would thrive. And yet we live in a society where people get beaten up—or worse—because they dare to assert an undeniable truth like the one this young man knew about himself. I know from talking with him the pain and anguish he went through to get to the place of being *him*. And yet he persisted.

There is something in the self that will not be denied. This was true for my student, and it's true for me. There are days that I think, *How did I get here? I must be damn lucky*. But then I remember the work, the tears, the counselors—some bad, many good—and the mentors. I remember my own dogged persistence. Instead of remaining in the closet and living a life pretending that I was someone I was not, I pushed myself down the path of living honestly. There was luck at times, and blind faith, and grace. Who knows? Maybe a stubbornness that I was born with, but there were things I cultivated, too.

I know Mom persisted as well, despite wanting to give up. Mom told me at one point that, according to what she was taught growing up, "girls don't brag and girls should be quiet." Instead of stifling her voice, she chose to write poetry. Many of her poems give voice to her aunts, her in-laws, and her grandmother, imagining a rich, inner world for women who lived and died without ever truly speaking their minds.

Mom also told me that "every step of the way seemed tentative and fraught with anxiety," and yet she moved with integrity and honesty to become a change agent in our family. In redefining the roles of daughter, wife, and mother, she helped the three men she loves the most to grow and become better husbands and fathers.

Mom wrote to me once that, when she was young, there was a certain amount of "fear of not being loved because you did not follow all the rules. And guilt because you did not follow all the rules." She went on to say, "But as I read long ago, and what has helped me immeasurably, is the belief that I will never be done with that fear and guilt. But I have to take steps to move on, despite it."

Mom has not only moved on. She has become an activist who attends PFLAG meetings and rallies for women's issues, writes letters to *The Buffalo News* criticizing the Catholic church and blog posts criticizing the pope and speaks out to all who will listen about love being love. She is an inspiration and a role model for her granddaughters Isabella and Zoe, and for their brothers Jordan and Noah, too.

For what seemed like the umpteenth time, I said to Mom, "No, really. This is your story as much as it is mine!"

In response, she said, "Part of me says, 'Who cares?'"

Mom's initial idea for this book was that it focus on me and my coming out. I think that in some ways she was still trying to fulfill the role of mother, putting me first, thinking of my bravery and not hers. What she had forgotten is that over the last many years, our relationship has expanded. We have inspired, cajoled, and encouraged bravery in one another. We are on this road together, sharing our journey.

Finding a path of persistence is difficult but worthy. For Mom and me, engaging in this writing process has been a reminder of where we come from. It also reminds us of where we are headed. We are reminded not only to stake our claim to the past but also to set our sights on where we will continue to roam.

Moving forward, we will keep paying attention to the truths that surface inside us—about ourselves and the world—and to how those truths can inform how we live. Holding tight to those we love, we take the next step....

ACKNOWLEDGEMENTS

Linda

First and foremost I have to thank my son Christopher who had the idea for the book more than ten years ago when he sent me for Mother's Day, *Not Like Other Boys: Growing Up Gay: A Mother and Son Look Back* by Marlene Fanta Shyer and Christopher Shyer. He said then we should do something like this. When I flagged and became discouraged he kept up my spirits. (Ok, sometimes he pushed, but never would I have continued without him.)

My son Mark was a great cheerleader to both of us on this journey. As a career journalist and editor he read the manuscript with a loving but critical eye. Bob read more drafts than I care to remember, but unfailingly persisted with his attentive care for those nasty typos and misspellings. He offered support by providing time to write while he made his famous meatloaf dinner or folded laundry. My son-in-law Patrick, despite being a busy assistant dean in the University of Washington College of Education, gave me such helpful responses especially on education.

There were the many dear friends who contributed to this endeavor:

Mary Callahan, who not only read this but who lived much of it with me. She and Marguerite Collesano have walked with me in our five plus decades of friendship.

Barbara Faust and Kathy Shoemaker who listened, read, and kept encouraging me, as they have for so many years. Jacyra Guard who gave not only friendship but excellent editorial feedback. The Women of the Crooked Circle and our dear Jimmie Gilliam who gave us our start on this path of writing together.

A big thank-you to Evelyn Brady who walked this path ahead of us and helped us on the way. Special thanks to Keith Elkins who went over the manuscript with his eagle eye—twice! And Nancy Parisi who took such great photos that you see on the back of the cover and on our web site. And Chet Syput who kept asking, "When's the book ready?"

Christopher

This book would never have come into existence without the encouragement and support of my dad and my brother. Although they are characters in this book, it is their book, too.

Judy Bromberek and Lillian Drawdy read an early draft and have been generous with their lives, love, and support. Your unconditional love from day one has meant the world to me. Diane Kendall, Chris Wenzler, and Edie Henderson also read early drafts and have helped to love this book into existence.

Thank you, thank you, thank you, Laurel Minter, for your insight, pep talks, and attaboys for years and years.

Jenn Hager, our amazing editor, helped to bring truth and clarity to the story we hoped to tell. Jessica Hatch also edited a final version, and we appreciate her keen eye and thoughtful suggestions. Thanks to Mark Pogodzinski at NFB Publishing for his belief in this book, and for supporting writers and their vision. Mark Figlozzi and Susan Jackson at Bizango offered invaluable assistance with all things marketing, and their generosity of time and expertise was amazing.

I owe so much to The Basics: Savanah Atabello, Kim Driscoll, Katherine Klekas, Tara Knudsen, David Lasby, Courtney Mack, Van Onishi, Amy Ries, Laura Streckenbach, and Carolyn Yuen.

Special thanks to my community of friends who have been a source of comfort and inspiration over many, many years: Doug McCrary, Paul Chiocco, Erin Katz, Siobhan Ring, Colette Ogle, Maura and Tom FitzMacken, Natalie and Jeff Lecher Pozarski, Gina and Chris Burns, Caitlin Coleman, Lisa Love, Jen Marlowe, Jeff Dolce, and Dennis Callahan. Thanks to Adrienne Romanowicz and Michele Gardner for your encouragement and support in getting the word out.

Isabella and Jordan provided many ideas on marketing, as well as countless thoughts about how to spend the royalties.

Patrick has been with me every step of the way, reading and rereading, encouraging and pressing, helping me to see that this was as much Mom's story as it was mine, and giving me the time and space to write. I could never have done this without you.

Mom, your courage is a continued source of inspiration, and I am so appreciative that we went on this journey together. What's next?

About the Authors

LINDA DRAJEM is a retired teacher. She taught high school English for over twenty-five years. After a late life Ph.D. from the University of Buffalo she taught for nine years in the English Education department at Buffalo State College. As a member of a long-standing writing group, Women of the Crooked Circle, she continues to write. She has been published in The Buffalo News and some literary journals. In addition, she has published a collection of poetry, *Arrows of Time*, and another, *InnerSessions*, with dear friends and poets Barbara Faust and Kathy Shoemaker. A teacher at heart, she is a docent at the Burchfield Penney Art Center and a presenter on literary topics at local senior centers. She and her husband Bob live in Buffalo, New York but often visit their sons, one on each coast. She loves the opportunity to be with her four fabulous grandchildren

CHRISTOPHER DRAJEM has been out to his parents since March of 1994. He met Patrick Sexton, the love of his life, in 1997, and married him on board a decommissioned Washington State ferry in August of 2001. In 2003 they adopted a daughter, Isabella, and in 2007 a son, Jordan. In January 2012, Patrick and Christopher were legally married in the state of Washington. They often travel to Buffalo and Long Island to visit family and friends. Christopher has remained involved with the adoption agency that facilitated their children's adoptions. In 2008, he teamed up with another adoptive parent to provide quarterly training for LGBTQ individuals and couples who are in the process of adopting. He has presented numerous workshops on LGBTQ inclusive curriculum in schools and is a proud member of the Bellevue-Eastside PFLAG. Christopher currently teaches high school English in Bellevue, Washington and likes to kayak and bake pies.

www.ingramcontent.com/pod-product-compliance
Lightning Source LLC
Chambersburg PA
CBHW070420010526
44118CB00014B/1838